The Shannon-Erne Waterway

For Mairéad

Above: The first boat through after the opening — from Lough Erne, leaving Lock No. 10, 3 April 1994.
Previous page: The approach to Lough Scur from the west, 3 April 1994.

The Shannon-Erne Waterway

Patrick Flanagan

Wolfhound Press

First published 1994 by WOLFHOUND PRESS Ltd
68 Mountjoy Square, Dublin 1

The publishers and the author gratefully acknowledge financial assistance from ESB towards the publication of this book.

Cover: front top, Approaching the new mooring at Leitrim (photo, the author). Main photo: Ballymagauran Lough with Garadice Lough in left background (photo ESBI). Back cover: New mooring at Haughton's Shore (Ballinacur) with inset Swans on Lough Scur (Photos ESBI).

A CIP catalogue record for this book is available from the British Library.

ISBN 0 86327 429 3
Typesetting: Wolfhound Press
Design: Jan de Fouw
Printed in the Republic of Ireland by Colour Books, Dublin

The Control Panel at Ballinamore Lock [No 6]

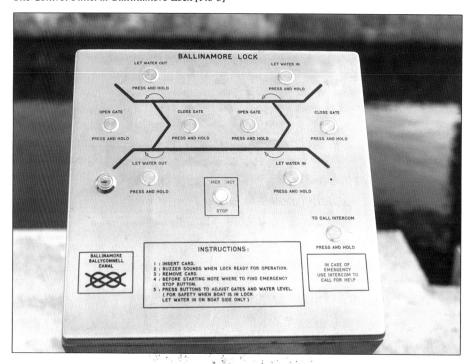

BtV

Contents

The Ruined Original Weir at Corraquill [Caroul]

Acknowledgements

My interest in the Ballinamore Canal grew out of an earlier investigation of the railway which served much the same region, and it was strongly encouraged by the Most Rev Dr F.J. McKiernan, Bishop of Kilmore, whose help was absolutely invaluable. In addition, he introduced me to various people whose knowledge of the canal was matched only by their hospitality. I am most grateful to him and to the many people who helped me, especially to Mr Paddy Quinn and to Mr John Edwards, who patiently answered my many questions and were most hospitable; to the Rev D. Gallogly, his brother, Joe, and his father, for their company on field trips, their hospitality, and their continued interest in my researches; to Professor and Mrs H.M. Power for their great assistance; to Dr D.B. McNeill, who gave me much help, particularly with the early references; to my brothers, Francis and John, for providing transport and company on field surveys; and to my parents for their great encouragement. Thanks are also due to Messrs A.L. Dowley and W. Levinge, and to Mr Charles Hadfield, who advised me throughout the writing of the original book.

I am grateful to the staffs of the National Library of Ireland and the Public Record Office of Ireland, and I thank the Director of the National Library and the Deputy Keeper of the Records for providing valuable source material. I am indebted to Joan McManus, who expertly typed the final version of the original text. In addition, she and her husband, Derry, were most generous in their hospitality and they offered many constructive and encouraging suggestions. I owe them both sincere thanks, as I do to Stephaney Bissett and Fiona Kennedy who most kindly prepared a computerised version of the earlier book to serve as a basis for much of the present volume.

Particular thanks are due to the Electricity Supply Board for their very generous support of the present volume. I would especially like to thank Mr Kieran O'Brien and Mr Larry Donald of the ESB for their unstinted assistance.

Lock No 5 at Ardrum in 1970

In compiling the second part of this book I have been aided greatly by three technical papers on the waterway delivered to the Institution of Engineers of Ireland by staff of the OPW and ESB International, and I would like to express my indebtedness to the authors. The papers were: *Ballinamore and Ballyconnell Canal: Feasibility of Restoration*, by John McHale, Brian Mangan and M.C. Martin, OPW, delivered in September 1988; *Reconstruction of the Ballinamore and Ballyconnell Canal*, by Thomas Bree and Brian O'Mahony, ESBI, delivered in March 1993; and *Geotechnical Aspects of the Reconstruction of the Ballinamore and Ballyconnell Canal*, by Michael M. Quigley and Kieran Creed, ESBI, delivered in February 1994. These sources were invaluable.

My thanks are due to ESB International for supplying a complete set of maps of the navigation which were of great assistance in the compilation of the gazetteer. ESBI also very kindly made available a selection of excellent photographs, several of which are reproduced here, and I would like to thank Mr Brian Murphy of ESBI for his help in this regard.

There are many other people to whom I am indebted. Among them are Messrs P. Corish and P. Pigott, of the OPW, for much valuable information. Mr John Carty, OPW, most kindly provided me with copies of the tolls and by-laws of the original navigation, which I had not previously seen. Special thanks are due to Brendan Pender and Herbert Richards for their help on a range of matters — transport, documentation, photography — and invaluable discussion on many topics. I owe particular thanks to Mr Brendan O'Donoghue.

Finally, I would like to acknowledge my debt to all who assisted in the production of this book — especially Mr Seamus Cashman and Ms Josephine O'Donovan of Wolfhound Press, and Mr Jan de Fouw, who undertook the design of the volume and who prepared the excellent maps. I would have been at a serious loss without their expertise, and it has been a great pleasure to have collaborated with them.

Introduction

The early 1990s is a time of unprecedented developments on Irish waterways. The highly improbable, if not seemingly impossible, is being achieved in several instances. The Royal Canal is being restored steadily and has already been opened to navigation from western Dublin to Mullingar; the River Suck is being made navigable to Ballinasloe; the navigation of the complete Shannon system will again be possible with the extension of the Lough Allen Canal into the lake of that name; reopening of the Kilbeggan Branch of the Grand Canal is under consideration [the Naas Branch has already been restored]; feasibility studies are in hand regarding the possible restoration of the Ulster Canal....

But pride of place goes beyond all question to the restoration of the link between the Erne and Shannon navigation systems — the waterway which meanders along the Cavan-Fermanagh border, through part of County Cavan and on through central County Leitrim to join the Shannon along the Leitrim-Roscommon border. Known variously as the 'Shannon-Erne' Waterway or Navigation, the 'Ballinamore & Ballyconnell' Canal or Navigation (from the two largest towns along its course) or, simply, as the 'Ballinamore Canal', this link saw in 1873 the last of the few boats ever to traverse it and it has lain derelict for almost 120 years.

Because of its moribund state and total lack of commercial success the existence of this Shannon-Erne link has remained largely unknown to the population outside the area through which it ran. But to the student of waterways it was once a key part of the grandiosely titled Limerick-Belfast navigation, even though this had a notional existence of a mere dozen or so years. In much more recent times, many a waterways enthusiast has looked at the current map of Irish navigations and noted in particular the 'missing link' between the Erne and Shannon systems which have developed in parallel highly successful pleasure cruiser enterprises. To link the two would surely be of great mutual benefit and give the country a unified waterways network, unrivalled in Europe as a cruising paradise.

The Ballinamore & Ballyconnell Canal is also known because of its relatively infamous history. It was never conceived as a straightforward canal but was instead designed as a 'navigation undertaken in connexion with drainage' under the drainage legislation of the early Victorian era. It came, very slowly, into existence as a mixture of still-water canal, a variety of lakes large and tiny, and river channel, which was beset by various problems virtually from the date of its 'completion'.

It is largely because of the range of factors involved, not least the inherent potential conflict between navigation, for which adequate water must be provided, and drainage, to which abundant water is anathema, that the term 'restoration' is inadequate to describe the enormous effort and multiplicity of works which constituted the creation of the 1994 Ballinamore & Ballyconnell Canal. The distinctive signs erected at key sites on the waterway proudly announced the 'reconstruction' of the navigation — and that is what it has been; no lesser term is adequate to describe the enormous project which has been magnificently carried out.

This book presents a concise history of the original navigation and its ignominious decline, alongside an account of the recent developments and a description of what has been achieved. The fact is that, what is very largely a new navigation, has been constructed in barely three years, albeit along a course with a rich history.

AUTHOR'S NOTE

The historical and much of the topographical content of this volume is based on my previous detailed history of the early Shannon-Erne Waterway, *The Ballinamore & Ballyconnell Canal*, published in 1972 by David & Charles, Newton Abbot, Devon, to whom grateful acknowledgement is made. The reader wishing to appreciate the minutiae of the conception, construction and decline of the original canal should consult this work.

This book condenses the detailed history in order to present a broad picture which would merge with an account of the astonishing rebirth of the Ballinamore Canal in the 1990s. Other than in direct quotations, all units are decimal or metric; within quotations the latter equivalents are given in brackets after the original units.

Placenames are given as formally adopted for the new waterway. As with the very name of the waterway, many locations along its course have in the past been [correctly] referred to by two or more names. I am using the official names with, where relevant, commonly used alternative names given in brackets.

LOCATION OF THE SHANNON-ERNE WATERWAY

SHANNON-ERNE WATERWAY

DERRY

ANTRIM

LARNE

LOUGH NEAGH

DONEGAL

BELFAST

LOWER L. ERNE

ENNISKILLEN

ERNE NAVIGATION

SLIGO

UPPER L. ERNE

BELTURBET

NEWRY

LOUGH ALLEN
LOUGH KEY

CARRICK-ON-SHANNON

DROGHEDA

KNOCK

LOUGH BOFIN

MULLINGAR

SHANNON NAVIGATION

DUBLIN

LOUGH REE

ATHLONE
GALWAY

PORTUMNA

TULLAMORE

KILDARE

SCARIFF

LOUGH DERG

CARLOW

ENNIS

KILLALOE

LIMERICK

WEXFORD

TRALEE

WATERFORD

ROSSLARE

CORK

 ⌒⌒⌒ *Navigable waterways*
 ‐‐‐‐ *closed to navigation*

PART ONE

THE ORIGINAL NAVIGATION

It is one of the most shameful pieces of mismanagement
in any country.

John Grey Vesey Porter, 1881

Cloncoohy Accommodation Bridge, pictured in 1947 [courtesy Mr J. Carty, OPW]

Notice of intention to enter and offer pending Proceedings to award Compensation.

DRAINAGE,

Acts 5th and 6th Vic., c. 89; 8th and 9th Vic., c. 69; 9th Vic., c. 4; and 10th and 11th Vic., c. 79.

District of *Ballinamore & Bally Connell*

WHEREAS, an Act was made and passed in the 5th and 6th years of the Reign of Her present Majesty, intituled "An Act to promote the Drainage of Lands, and improvement of Navigation and Water Power in connexion with such Drainage in Ireland." And whereas another Act was made and passed in the 8th and 9th years of the Reign of Her said present Majesty, intituled, "An Act to amend the Act of the 6th year of Her present Majesty, for promoting the Drainage of Lands, and improvement of Navigation and Water Power in connexion with such Drainage in Ireland." And whereas a certain other Act was passed in the 9th year of the Reign of Her said present Majesty, intituled, "An Act to amend the Acts for promoting the Drainage of Lands, and improvement of Navigation and Water Power in connexion with such Drainage in Ireland, and to afford facilities for increased employment for the labouring classes in Works of Drainage, during the present year."

Now, in pursuance of the provisions in said Acts, or some of them, contained, We, the Commissioners of Public Works in Ireland, acting in the execution of the said Acts, hereby give you notice that it is our intention by our Engineers, Workmen, and other persons, after the expiration of three days from the date of the service of this Notice, to enter in and upon all that and those *The Lands of Drumany O'Brien in the Barony of Mohill and County of Leitrim*

for the purpose of executing the necessary Works by the said Acts authorized, within the District denominated by us the District of *Ballinamore & Bally Connell* in the Counties of *Cavan Fermanagh Leitrim & Roscommon* and doing any other act, matter, or thing, requisite, in our opinion, for fully carrying into effect the purposes of the said Acts, within said District, and pending the proceedings taken by us for the purpose of examining, assessing, and awarding, what sum of money should be paid by us for the recompense, satisfaction, or compensation to be allowed for any damage or injury to said Lands, Tenements, and Premises, respectively, we hereby offer you the sum of *One Shilling*

for such recompense, satisfaction, or compensation, which sum we will, (if you agree to accept same,) apportion and pay in accordance with your respective Estates and Interests in said Lands and Premises.

Dated at the Office of Public Works, Custom House, Dublin, this *Tenth* day of *April* 18*72*

Radcliff
W. T. Mulvany

} Two of the Commissioners of Public Works In Ireland.

To
The Proprietor or Proprietors, Lessees, and Occupiers, and all other persons interested in the said Lands and Premises above-mentioned.

By Authority—ALEX. THOM, 87, Abbey-street, Dublin.

A 'Three-Day Notice' of intention to enter lands, offering one shilling [5p] compensation

CHAPTER 1

THE BACKGROUND

The Ballinamore & Ballyconnell Navigation was built primarily to link two of the more important Irish rivers — the Erne, which flows roughly north-west through Counties Cavan and Fermanagh to the Atlantic at Ballyshannon, in south County Donegal, and the Shannon, which rises in County Cavan and flows south for over 160 kilometres to the sea at Limerick City. By the 1840s, when the scheme for the Ballinamore Canal was conceived and implemented, the development of the principal inland navigations of Ireland was virtually complete. From the Erne it was possible to reach Belfast and Newry by water, while the Shannon was doubly linked to Dublin, via the midlands, by the Royal and Grand Canals. Thus the completion of this link of some sixty kilometres would unify the waterway network.

Of the 60-odd kilometres of the Ballinamore Canal, some 8 consist of a still-water navigation, 13 lie through lakes and the rest comprise the canalized course of the Woodford River. About 35 kilometres lie wholly in Leitrim, 13 in Cavan and the rest form either the Fermanagh/Cavan or Cavan/Leitrim boundary. The first 10 kilometres of the navigation from Lough Erne run virtually entirely along the boundary between Cavan and Fermanagh, which is also the Border between Ireland and Northern Ireland.

Commencing at a point about 6 kilometres north of the town of Belturbet the navigation runs south-west for 5 kilometres to Aghalane, where it turns to head north-west for 3 kilometres. Beyond Corraquill it resumes its south-westerly course and after 5 kilometres passes the town of Ballyconnell. Eight kilometres further on the waterway enters a chain of lakes — Coologe, Derrycassan and Ballymagauran [Ballymagovern] — flowing in a more westerly direction. Leaving Ballymagauran Lake it passes Woodford Demesne and enters Garadice Lake, the largest on the system with an area of some 450 hectares [1,100 acres]. Although the western outfall of Garadice Lake is only 5 kilometres from Ballinamore, the canal takes a U-shaped course of some 7 kilometres to reach the town.

Heading north out of Ballinamore the canal soon turns west and runs to

DRAINAGE.

Under the Act 5th and 6th Vic., Ch. 89.

DISTRICT OF
BALLINAMORE & BALLYCONNELL,
COUNTIES LEITRIM, CAVAN, and FERMANAGH.

NOTICE is hereby given, that COPIES of the PRELIMINARY REPORT on the proposed Drainage of the FLOODED LANDS in the District of Ballinamore and Ballyconnell, in the counties of Leitrim, Cavan, and Fermanagh. and on the Line of the Junction Navigation for connecting Lough Erne and the River Shannon, required to be made under the provisions of the Act 5th and 6th Victoria, c. 89, HAVE BEEN DEPOSITED with the Clerks of the Peace, and Secretaries of the Grand Juries of the Counties Leitrim, Cavan, and Fermanagh, respectively and copies of said Report have also been deposited with Mrs Willes, White Hart Hotel, Enniskillen ; Mr E. Fitzpatrick, Hotel, Belturbet ; Mr H Church, Hotel, Carrick on-Shannon : Mr Thos. Nugent, Hotel, Swanlinbar ; Mr D. Thompson, Hotel, Ballinamore ; and Mr Patrick Kane, Hotel, Ballyconnell, to remain open for public inspection for six successive weeks, as by said Act required, and copies of said Report may be obtained on application at any of the above-mentioned hotels, or at the Office of Public Works, Custom House, Dublin. for the sum of Sixpence each.

By Order of the Commissioners.

HENRY R. PAINE, Secretary.

Dated at the Office of Public Works,
Custom House, Dublin, this
7th day of August 1845.

Notice of Completion of Preliminary Report on the Drainage Proposals
Another view of Cloncoohy Accommodation Bridge 1947 — see p.11 above

Creevy, a distance of about 3 kilometres. Here the navigation turns south-west again and, following a new channel, comes to St John's Lough about 1.5 kilometres further on. This 'lake' is in fact a series of three small lakes and the navigation threads southwards through them to Muckros where it diverges west for 2.5 kilometres along the old course of the Aghacashlaun River to Castlefore.

Again the waterway heads south-west, along what is virtually a new cut, through Lough Marrave, into Lough Scur. From this lake, which is the central point of the summit level, the navigation runs south-west for some 8 kilometres to the Shannon, just beyond Leitrim village. This last section is virtually a pure still-water canal, although near Leitrim the Black Lough and the Leitrim River were incorporated into its course.

The region through which the canal flows is characterized by a great number of small lakes and low hills, although there is some high ground to the north of its course. Ballyconnell lies at the foot of 'the bleak, barren and lofty range of the Slieve Russell mountains' while the canal is fed by the rivers rushing down from the range of the Aghacashel Mountains, the principal peaks of which are Slieve Anierin (586 metres), Slievenakilla (547 metres), Gubnaveagh (520 metres) and Benbrack (502 metres).

The land served by the canal is poor and nowadays greatly depopulated, and Ballinamore and Ballyconnell are the only significant towns along the route, though they could never have been considered large. The latter had a population of around 400 in the 1840s but Ballinamore was nearly twice the size, and was distinguished by its important market and its 'remarkably clean, airy, comfortable and prosperous appearance'. Two other small towns lie on or near the canal — Keshcarrigan, near Castlefore, described in 1846 as a 'poor, squalid place', and Leitrim village, of which it was remarked at that time too that it was 'so unpeopled and deserted, that scarce one remains there to tell anything about it'.

Early Proposals

This was hardly promising country for a canal and were it not for the benefits expected from a Shannon-Erne link it would never have been built. Various factors contributed to the birth of the Ballinamore Canal, all of them culminating in the proceedings of the mid-1840s. However, there had been much earlier suggestions for a navigation of a very similar nature.

Towards the end of the 1770s interest awakened in the north-west. The canal engineer, Richard Evans, developed a plan for quite an extensive navigation and parliamentary approval was granted in 1778. Starting from a sea terminal at Murray's Quay in Ballyshannon, a canal would run close to the unnavigable Erne for some 8 kilometres to Belleek. Past the falls above Belleek, the canal would enter Lower Lough Erne, through which lake a navigable channel would be made to Enniskillen. From there the navigation would continue through Upper Lough Erne to Belturbet. Short of that town there would be a branch navigation along the Woodford River to Ballyconnell, with a possible future extension to Ballinamore, Lough Scur and the Shannon at Leitrim.

Work on the scheme commenced in 1780 and later men were at work along part of the route of the Ballinamore Canal. However, the work was beset by financial problems in 1786, and all works had been stopped by 1792. By then a lock was half built at Corraquill [Caroul], and a lock house had been erected.

In April 1793 came a report from William Chapman of Newcastle 'On the means of making Woodford River navigable from Lough-Erne to Woodford-Lough'. Chapman thought that there were no insurmountable difficulties and that for £5,000 a navigation could be made from Woodford [Garadice] Lough to Lough Erne. The principal features of his proposed navigation were locks at Aghalane Bridge, at 'the rapids at Curhoul' [Corraquill, where a lock was nearly complete], at Ballyconnell, at Ballyheady Bridge, and at the outfall of Coologe Lough [near Kiltynaskellan (Skelan) Ford]. There would be new bridges at Aghalane and Ballyheady locks, and expenditure at Ballyconnell would be reduced by making use of the head-race for the mill instead of following the river course proper.

He thought that the navigation should be capable of handling boats from 10 to 20 tonnes, drawing 2-2.5ft [0.6-0.75m] in summer and up to 4ft [1.2m] of water in winter. For haulage he felt that a 'narrow path for men' would suffice, as there would be much difficulty in providing a horse towing path because neither side of the river was 'favourable for a track-way for the whole length'.

It is a little difficult to understand Chapman's recommendation that the navigation be extended as far west as Garadice Lake, for there could have been little hope of any worthwhile traffic from the few scattered hamlets in the region. However, he certainly considered an extension to the Shannon. From Garadice it was over 6.5 kilometres to Ballinamore, though this could be cut by 1.5 kilometres if a canal were built.

From Ballinamore, Chapman wrote, it was

> just two miles [3km] further to the outlet of the Lough of Ballyduff, from whence it is Navigable by a chain of small Lakes to the west end of the Lough north of Kishcarrigan; from which, a Canal of about four miles [6.5km] in length, would pass through favourable ground in the vale north of Sheebeg, and onwards to the Shannon at Leitrim.

In other words he mapped out fairly closely the course of the navigation made a half-century later. In one respect, however, Chapman was more than a little wide of the mark in his prediction

> Not having ascertained the quantity of rise and fall in this line, I can't take upon myself to say further, than that the expense will be moderate, compared both with the distance and the object.

Chapman thought that the possibility of the link with the Shannon would stimulate practical interest in the Woodford-Lough Erne navigation, but he was convinced that the scheme then in hand could not proceed unless the Ballyshannon-Belleek link were completed. In the preceding years work had also been done on this latter canal; earthworks had been carried out and one lock, of a projected twelve, was built near Belleek. But in 1794 funds ran out; the scheme expired and with it died the Woodford River project.

In 1801 the newly-established Directors-General of Inland Navigation asked Evans to submit a revised estimate. His reply was that the original sum of £40,000 — for the combined navigations — should be increased to £48,000 but once again no funds were forthcoming and the plans were dropped, the partly completed works being abandoned for good.

In 1831 the first Commissioners of Public Works in Ireland were appointed and entrusted with the powers of the directors general of inland navigation. This new body, then known as the Board of [Public] Works, but nowadays as the Office of Public Works [OPW], was later to play the leading role in the early history of the Ballinamore Canal. In the same year a commission was appointed to investigate the Shannon navigation. The first Shannon Navigation Act was passed in 1835 and more commissioners were appointed, charged with the duty of preparing plans and surveys for the improvement of the Shannon.

William Mulvany Investigates

The question of a Shannon-Erne link was not overlooked in the planning for the improvement of the Shannon. The preparatory commission of 1835 raised the topic after a reference had been made to it by the Treasury. W.T. Mulvany, a civil engineer employed by the commission, was instructed to report on the practicability of making such a link and to examine the terrain between the Shannon at Drumsna and the Erne at Belturbet or 'the point near Wattle Bridge, where the Ulster Canal is to open into the River Erne'. The Ulster Canal Company had itself financed surveys of more or less the same territory in 1837-8 with a view to the future extension of its navigation.

Mulvany's report was dated 11 March 1839 and it stated that he had:

> perambulated the whole line of summit southwards through the County of Leitrim into the County of Longford, where it terminates in the high hills south east of Ballinamuck.

The terrain, although not mountainous in general, was dotted with hills and Mulvany was primarily concerned with finding a suitable summit level for a canal. He came up with three possibilities, the favoured one being the pass at Letterfine near Lough Scur, which he termed the 'Ballinamore Line'. The summit level was at 220ft [67m] OD [above Ordnance Datum], necessitating about 15 locks, and its catchment was such as to provide an adequate water supply 'without the construction of supply courses or other expensive works'.

The line was very similar to that proposed by Chapman 45 years earlier, leaving the Shannon at Leitrim village, 'at the harbour proposed to be formed by the Shannon Commissioners,' and running along the valley of the Leitrim River to Letterfine, 'where the average depth of cutting to obtain the required supply would be but 13 feet 6 inches [4.1m], for a length of 2,400 yards [2200m]'. From this summit the canal would be laid out 'under all the advantageous circumstances of gradually falling ground, through the valley of Ballinamore, to join the River Erne, a little above the town of Belturbet', and the way to the Ulster Canal would then be via a proposed lock in Belturbet.

Mulvany had a general knowledge of the country through which the line would run but, as he had not 'perambulated it in detail', he was not very specific about the route east of Ballinamore and he spelt out two possibilities — a canal to Killeshandra, whence the river would be followed to Belturbet, or the length of river navigation could be reduced to 1.5 kilometres by 'the construction of 4 additional miles [6.5 km] of Canal in the direct line'. In either case he felt that the line via Ballinamore would be the most suitable from both commercial and engineering points of view.

It had been part of Mulvany's brief to report on the 'Traffic and the Amount of Commercial Benefit' likely to arise if a canal were built and the latter part of his report was devoted to this aspect. Newry and Belfast were then the chief trading ports for the countryside between the Erne and Letterfine (itself only 5 miles [8km] from the Shannon), and to 'Ballinamore, within 14 miles [22.5km] of the Shannon, even the heavy article of timber is frequently brought by land carriage from Newry and Belfast'. Even towns like Mohill and Boyle which would have much trade with Dublin would still be expected to send much of their livestock and agricultural produce to the north along the proposed canal.

A list of specific traffics which Mulvany thought would materialise included coal 'from the Arigna and other Collieries in the neighbourhood of Lough Allen', iron 'from Arigna to the foundries at Belfast and the North of Ireland', livestock and so on. The report noted that slates and marble from Killaloe 'may be expected to be sent through this canal to the North', and Mulvany, while not venturing a precise estimate of the traffic, was of the firm opinion that the canal would be of a 'remunerative nature'.

Although the relative haste with which the investigation was made precluded Mulvany from making any sort of detailed survey of the country through which the Ballinamore line would run, he did not overlook the all-important question of cost. Taking as the basis for his calculations 'the full cost, per mile, of the Ulster Canal, inclusive of very heavy Parliamentary expenses' — which he hoped would 'in future be avoided in works of Public utility' — Mulvany set out the probable cost:

28.5 miles [45.5km] of canal, including Locks, Bridges &c., at £5,000 per mile	£142,500
Lock, regulating Weir, and other works at Belturbet, say	£ 10,000
Shoal between Belturbet and terminus of Ulster Canal, say	£ 500
	———
Total for Canal from Leitrim to Belturbet, and thence to Ulster Canal	£153,000
Probable cost of removing Shoals, altering Bridges, and improving navigation for steam vessels from Belturbet by the River Erne and Lough Oughter to Killeshandra	£ 14,000
	———
	£167,000

Mulvany concluded his report with the remark that were the proposed Shannon works to be carried out, the advantages of the junction canal would be very considerable and 'perhaps render it deserving of a proportionate share of public support and control'. In the event of the Shannon works not being undertaken he felt the canal would carry the whole trade of the region it served and that this would 'probably... render it a fit speculation for private enterprise.' If the latter were the case he thought most of the traffic would go on through the Ulster Canal and that then the locks on the junction canal needed only to be built to the smaller dimensions of the former waterway. But he added a rider:

> ...As the projects for the improvement of the Upper Shannon are now under the consideration of the Legislature, and it is to be presumed will soon be carried into effect, and as the additional expenditure which would be incurred in adopting the larger scale of the Royal and Grand Canals would not be considerable, and would arise chiefly from a small increase in the size of the locks, it seems desirable that the grand object of making this a Junction Canal common to all the principal navigations of Ireland, should not, on account of this additional expenditure, be lost to the public.

However, Mulvany's report evidently met with a lack of interest as no action was taken on it and the idea was shelved. Possibly the Treasury remained unconvinced of the value which might be returned on the expenditure of a sum nearly a third of that budgeted for the works along the whole Shannon. But the project was soon to come to the fore again, the stimulus coming from the passing of an Act in 1842.

E S T I M A T E

OF THE EXPENCE

OF A PROPOSED NAVIGATION,

FROM *L O U G H   E R N E*

To *W O O D F O R D   L O U G H.*

	£.	s.	d.
Four Locks of 63 feet between the Gates, 12½ width of chamber and of various falls, at £.350	1400	0	0
Bridges over the Locks at Aughaline and Ballyheady,	120	0	0
Removing the Bar below Mullinacough and two shoals below Aughaline-bridge,	150	0	0
Deepening the shoals at Kilcorby and at the Eel Weir at Curhoul,	80	0	0
Finishing the Canal and Weir at Curhoul,	270	0	0
Making a Channel within the Island opposite Annagh Wood, and removing all obstructions to as far as the great Island below Ballyconnel,	75	0	0
Five miles of Trackway from the junction of Woodford River with the Erne, 2 miles of which I suppose high enough, and the rest to average 2 feet height, which with sodding may amount to 4s. 8d. per Perch, or 74l. 13s. 4d. per Mile,	224	0	0

William Chapman's Estimates for his Proposed Navigation of 1793

	£.	s.	d.
Canal above and below the Lock at Ballyconnel Mills, -	110	0	0
Deepening the Mill-courfe and repairing the Weir, -	80	0	0
Deepening and contracting the fhallow parts of the River between Ballyconnel and Ballyheady, about	400	0	0
600 Perches of Trackway, at an average of 5s. per, -	150	0	0
Canal at Ballyheady and alterations of the Weir, - - -	140	0	0
Deepening and contracting various parts of the River between Ballyheady and Curleach, -	160	0	0
500 Perches of Trackway, at 5s. per,	125	0	0
Canal at Curleach, - -	90	0	0
Towing Paths on the communications between the Loughs of Curleach, Burren, Ballymagauran and Woodford, about 200 Perches, at an average of 10s. per Perch,	100	0	0
Making a deep channel through the Eel Weir below Mr. Gore's, deepening the channel into Woodford Lough, and making a Navigation Arch in the Bridge,	250	0	0
Boats and Machinery,	150	0	0
	4374	0	0
Incidents and Superintendance, 15 per Cent.	655	7	0
	£.5029	7	0

Legislative Progress

The first Navigation Act, passed in 1715, included the important topic of land drainage in its scope, and interest was to focus repeatedly on the drainage question. Various moves were made to encourage the improvement of land by drainage, chief among them being the appointment of Commissioners of Bog Improvement, who held office from September 1807 until December 1813. Their efforts cost £37,221 and their findings were enshrined in voluminous reports but, unhappily, no actual works of drainage were carried out.

The position was unchanged up to the 1840s, but 1842 saw the passing of the Act 5 & 6 Vic, c 89 — the basic Act of the code of Irish arterial drainage law. Enacted on 5 August 1842, this Act stimulated a vast programme of arterial drainage works undertaken by the OPW, which was appointed the commissioners for its execution. Its relevance in the context of waterways is expressed in its title — 'An Act to promote the Drainage of Lands, and Improvement of Navigation and Water Power in connection with such Drainage, in Ireland'. This first Act formed the base on which a very limited number of navigations, including the Ballinamore Canal, were made.

The Act specified the procedures which were to be followed by persons interested in drainage or navigation projects. On receipt of a memorial from such persons the OPW would direct 'some Engineer or other competent Person' to survey the area and to investigate the proposals for drainage [and possibly navigation], taking note of the probable benefits to be derived from any work. Mills were also to be considered both from the point of view of acquiring and improving them. The inspector would report as to the probable expense of the proposed works.

The next stage was the making of a much more detailed survey of the proposed improvement area, showing the lands which would be improved by drainage and the cost of the works involved, and also 'the Proportions in which such Lands shall contribute towards the payment of the Costs'. The estimated navigation costs would be shown separately and the 'District likely to be benefited by such Improvement' and the 'Baronies, Half-Baronies or Townlands' which would have to bear the cost would also be specified.

In the case of proposed navigation works the grand juries of the district 'likely to be benefited' were empowered to approve the works and to undertake to pay their cost. No work was to start until such a declaration had been received from the county authorities and the payment of at least two-thirds of the estimated cost guaranteed by grand jury presentment.

Once the various administrative procedures had been completed the OPW made a formal declaration of the extent of the lands to be improved, their present and increased value after drainage, the charge to be levied on them and their proprietors. This declaration was vitally important. It also specified the proposed navigation improvements, setting out the district which would

SCHEDULE A—continued.

LANDS CHARGEABLE.

No. of sheet of Ordnance Map on which Lot is represented.	No. of Lot on Map, same number to same property.	Reputed Proprietors.	Townlands (as named on Ordnance Maps) chargeable.	Barony in which Townlands are situate.	County in which Townlands are situate.	Area of lands within one mile of the lands drained or improved, belonging to the same proprietors as the lands drained or improved, Statute Measure. A. R. P.	Area of lands drained or improved, Statute Measure. A. R. P.	Original value of lands drained and improved. £ s. d.	Annual Increase in the original value of lands drained and improved. £ s. d.	Proportion in which the sum numbered... (Decimals)	Amount of each half-yearly instalment of principal and interest, payable in respect of the several parcels or portions of the lands charged. £ s. d.	Rate to be levied and expended by Trustees, for first year's maintenance of Works. £ s. d.
38, 41			Aghinlisert,	Knockninny,	Fermanagh		25 2 30		6 0 10	Decimals.		
38, 41			Derrintony,	Do.,	Do.,		25 1 30		4 11 1			
38, 41	21	Collins, Dr. Robert,	Derryart,	Do.,	Do.,	663 3 33	27 2 20	44 16 7	6 12 3	·01515	12 14 2	1 1 3
41			Garvary,	Do.,	Do.,		30 1 10		6 0 2			
41			Unnera,	Do.,	Do.,		10 3 30		3 5 8			
9	22	Connolly, Thomas and Rev. Richard,	Killoogh,	Tullyhaw,	Cavan,	160 0 23	18 3 20	8 3 3	4 19 7	·00285	2 7 8	0 4 0
27	23	Crawford, M.	Tullyhunan (part of),	Leitrim,	Leitrim,	—	3 3 10	1 14 3	1 2 10	·00365	0 10 11	0 0 11
13	24	Dobbin, Leonard,	Kilnavert,	Tullyhaw,	Cavan,	430 2 31	11 3 10	38 3 6	1 11 1	·01333	11 7 0	0 18 11
9, 13			Port,	Do.,	Do.,		21 0 0		22 2 0			
9, 13	25	Dolan, James and Farrell,	Drumbarpher (part of),	Do.,	Leitrim,	110 0 0	4 2 20	2 15 9	1 17 0	·00106	0 17 10	0 1 6
24	26	Duckworth, Captain John,	Aghacashlaun,	Leitrim,	Leitrim,	179 2 30	27 1 10	7 18 0	3 11 1	·00348	2 18 5	0 4 10
24			Drumgad,	Do.,	Do.,		7 3 10		2 10 9			
38	27	Dunne, George N.,	Drunany More,	Knockninny,	Fermanagh,	171 3 1	27 0 30	11 12 1	9 7 3	·00535	4 9 10	0 7 6
9	28	Elliott, Mrs Jane,	Tiranwannagh,	Tullyhaw,	Cavan,	330 3 17	6 3 30	2 1 7	2 1 7	·00119	1 0 0	0 1 8
13	29	Ellis, Rev. Arthur,	Ballymagauran (pt. of),	Do.,	Do.,	259 2 29	21 1 0	43 8 0	9 10 6	·01767	14 16 0	1 4 9
13			Gortaclogher,	Do.,	Do.,		75 0 0		21 7 0			
24	29*	Do.,	Corlough,	Leitrim,	Leitrim,	14 2 0	2 0 0	0 10 0	0 7 0	·00020	0 3 4	0 0 8

A Page of Schedule A of the Final Drainage Award, setting out the proportions in which lands
would be charged

benefit from the work and which would pay for it, and also giving the details of any mills which would be interfered with by the work. If there were no appeals against the proposals, the OPW then published a 'final notice' stating that all the requirements of the Act had been fully complied with. The publication of the final notice was conclusive.

Further legislation was passed in 1845 and 1846 to streamline the complex procedures. The first Act of 1846 touched on navigation matters, the principal feature being that Parliament could grant 'a Moiety or more of the Expense' of making the navigation, while a second Act of that year made 'Provisions of a more summary Nature...whereby remunerative Employment [might] be afforded to the labouring Classes' on purely drainage works. Another Act was passed in July 1847 and it also reflected the then critical state of the Irish nation — this was the time of the Great Famine. This short Act also fixed very definitely the responsibilities of the grand juries of a navigation district to pay the rest of the cost outstanding after a free grant had been made. The charges necessary were to be levied directly off the area without the usual grand jury presentments being made.

This series of Acts formed the basic code of drainage/navigation law and, although further Acts were to be passed nearly a decade later, it was according to them that the OPW energetically began a programme of drainage schemes throughout the country. One of the major projects was in the Ballinamore & Ballyconnell District.

The Old Lock at Ballyduff [No 7]

CHAPTER 2

THE CONSTRUCTION PERIOD

The inception of the Ballinamore and Ballyconnell drainage and navigation project was a lengthy and highly complicated process. It was the 1842 Act which stimulated the landowners of Leitrim and Cavan to make a request for a drainage scheme, but the impetus for a navigation project came from another event of 1842 — the completion of the 46-mile Ulster Canal. The Ulster Canal Company was very anxious to extend westwards to the Shannon. Consequently it was not long before a memorial from the UCC reached the OPW.

The first moves, however, were for a drainage scheme. In 1844 the OPW received memorials from the landed proprietors seeking a drainage scheme to improve lands between Ballinamore and Ballyheady Bridge and from Ballyheady to Ballyconnell. Later the area was extended to 'the site of the old lock at Corquill,' and then about the beginning of September 1844 a request came from 'the proprietors of land adjoining the rivers and lakes near Keshcarrigan and Ballinamore,...for the drainage of lands in that locality as a continuation of the Ballinamore Drainage'. Finally, in November 1844, John McMahon, the OPW engineer then busy in the region east of Ballinamore, was told 'to take the necessary steps to have the inquiry extended accordingly from Lough Erne to the Shannon at Leitrim'.

McMahon was told that it seemed likely that the Woodford River could be followed for all but about 8km of the route and he was directed to pay special attention to land drainage west of Lough Scur, where a canal would be needed, and also to the control of the mountain rivers from the viewpoints of flood control and of providing a water supply for the navigation and the mills along its course. He was informed that the navigation 'should be suited to small class steamers worked either by paddles placed at the stern or the screw propeller' and he was warned to be economical. To complete his task he was required to afford information on the utility of the navigation as a link waterway and to give 'fullest information' on local traffic prospects.

By May 1845 McMahon's report was ready. It spelt out the probable costs of both the drainage and the navigation between the Shannon and the Erne.

The former was estimated to be £23,267, the latter £103,000, but he thought that if the works were executed jointly the aggregate cost would fall to £110,301. The OPW approved the report and its proposals and on 27 June wrote to the interested parties stating that the works would be executed jointly for drainage and navigation.

A letter was also sent to Roscommon Grand Jury noting that there was 'reason to hope that the benefits to be derived from the works... may extend to that county'. This was an interesting move and was possibly made as a 'softening-up' of the grand jury of a county through which the navigation would at no point pass and which would derive absolutely no benefit from the drainage measures. However, if the navigation were the success expected, then it would surely bring some benefit, possibly even leading to a revival of the fortunes of the Arigna coal and iron district, situated in that county.

Thereafter, however, there were various delays in the proceedings and the formal final notice of intent to proceed [initially with the drainage works] was not issued until 26 June 1846. Under it the way was clear for the drainage to be commenced; work commenced on 30 June in charge of William Forsyth. The OPW next dealt with the navigation proceedings. On the important question of finance the Treasury had helped. By a 'minute of 20 March 1846 [it] approved of granting a moiety of the cost peculiar to navigation'. The grant was made in response to a request from the Irish administration and the Cavan Grand Jury.

The sum was subsequently fixed at £46,250, 'the moiety without interest of the estimated cost'. An apportionment was then made of 'the other moiety or £49,625' over those areas of Cavan, Leitrim, Fermanagh and Roscommon which were deemed to be the beneficiaries of the navigation. On 4 March 1847 McMahon gave his final estimate of £131,858, based on his detailed design; it was made up as follows:

Drainage works — chargeable to proprietors	£ 27,110
Drainage — works of masonry in connection therewith, chargeable to counties	£ 4,582
Navigation works — chargeable to Government grant and to four counties	£100,166
	£131,858

Further procedural delays ensued and at one stage the drainage works were interrupted for financial reasons. However, the final 'all-clear' was given on 19 November 1847 for the navigation work to begin.

Construction Begins

For well over a year effort was concentrated on the drainage measure, the work affording 'a large amount of relief by reproductive employment'. Many hundreds of labourers were employed. Their equipment was primitive —

BOARD OF PUBLIC WORKS.

DRAINAGE and NAVIGATION.

Under the Acts 5th & 6th Vict, chap 89—8th & 9th Vic, chap 69—
9th Vic, chap 4—and 10th & 11th Vic, chap 79.

DISTRICT of BALLINAMORE and
BALLYCONNELL,
in the COUNTIES of CAVAN, FERMANAGH,
LEITRIM, and ROSCOMMON.

FINAL NOTICE
Of Compliance
with the requisites of the above mentioned Acts.

We, the Commissioners of Public Works in Ireland, acting in
execution of the above mentioned Acts, do hereby notify and
declare, that the several Preliminary Measures and Proceedings
by the Act of the 5th and 6th Vict, chap 89, entitled " An Act
to promote the Drainage of Lands, and Improvement of Navigation and Water Power in connexion with such Drainage in Ireland," and the several Acts amending the same, directed
to be taken and observed, previously to the commencement of
the proposed Works in the District of Ballinamore and Ballyconnell, in the counties of Cavan, Fermanagh, Leitrim, and
Roscommon. HAVE BEEN CONCLUDED. And we do
hereby GIVE THIS FINAL NOTICE, that all the requi-
sitions of the said Acts with respect to the lands within the said
District proposed to be Drained and Improved, and also with
respect to the making and improving of Navigation within
said District HAVE BEEN COMPLIED WITH.

> HARRY D. JONES } Two of the Commissioners of
> THOS A. LARCOM } Public Works in Ireland.

Dated at the Office of Public Works,
Custom House, Dublin,
this 19th day of November 1847.

Final Notice of Completion of the Initial Procedures for both Drainage and Navigation Works barrows, picks and shovels — and it was supplemented in December 1847 by further quantities of similar tools provided from the famine relief stores at Belturbet, Cavan, Sligo, Enniskillen and Swanlinbar.

The following years saw much interrupted progress, especially on the drainage works the benefits of which were soon apparent. But a combination of lack of funds, periods of abnormal rainfall, shortages of labour when harvest-time weather was fine, and occasional technical difficulties meant that overall progress on the works was slow. Nonetheless, by the end of 1849 the main channel was in an advanced state, the stretch from Ballyconnell to the Erne being nearly finished. In the reaches from Garadice to St John's Lough and from Drumany to Lough Scur, as well as on almost the whole length of the new navigation cut from Lough Scur to Leitrim, progress was good and it was anticipated that all the earthwork would be finished early in 1850.

Satisfaction was expressed with the progress at the most difficult spot — the heavy rock cutting on the summit level at Letterfine, west of Lough Scur. Work had also continued on the main channel on filling in the gaps along the route, at Ballyheady, the Aghoo/Ballinamore reach, and near Castlefore. In addition, the 'course of the river between Lough Marrave and Lough Scur, which was exceedingly swampy, [was] carefully drained and consolidated preparatory to the excavation of the navigable channel'.

Work continued throughout 1851 and 1852 at places where there were shoals — Coologe, Skelan, Woodford and Ballyconnell — and by the end of the latter year the Letterfine cut was complete, bringing to a virtual conclusion the work on the artificial cut from Lough Scur to the Shannon. By this time, too, excavation had given way to dredging, along the main channel. In 1852 it was reported that 'a large steam dredger', had been built at Belturbet and 'launched and fitted with steam engine, boiler and other machinery'. It was soon to prove very useful in dredging principally in the Coologe-Ballyconnell-Aghalane region.

Quite a number of completely new road bridges had to be built over the new navigation cuts and on the new courses of the feeder rivers, as did smaller accommodation bridges across the main channel and over lateral drainage channels at places where lands had been severed or where old fords had been swept away. Finally, there were the bridges over the river courses involved in the navigation, which had existed long before the commencement of the works but which required alteration or reconstruction. In the first six years of the works some 20 bridges were built or completely rebuilt. Most were fine masonry structures, though some of the smaller accommodation bridges were either of timber or wrought iron executed at the Belturbet workshops set up in 1850.

Lock construction began in 1848 along the river section of the navigation and at each of the eight locations a weir had also to be built. Provision had also to be made for large sluices beside the weirs to permit the rapid discharge of

Showing the relative CAPABILITIES (in an Engineering point of view) of the several Lines, examined for the purposes of a proposed JUNCTION CANAL, between the RIVERS SHANNON and ERNE.

Description of Line.	Length in Statute Miles.	Height of proposed Summit Level above the Sea.	Total Rise and Fall.	Deepest Cutting at Summit.	Rate of Lockage per Statute Mile.	No. of Locks required.	Area of Catchment Basin for supply of Summit Level.	Observations.
		Feet.	Feet.	Ft. In.	Ft.Dec.		Statute Acres.	
THE BALLINAMORE LINE, {Canal, - 28¼ / River, - 1}	29¼	220	150	23 0	5.00	16	10,320, including 670 of Lakes, -	See Fig. No. 1, Sheet of Sections.
Do., by Killeshandra, {Canal, - 24¼ / River & Lake, 14}	38¼	220	150	Do.	5.75	16	Do. Do.	Do. Do.
THE MOHILL LINE, (examined by the Ulster Canal Company,) - - -	30	239	196	31 6	6.53	21	970, including 48 acres of Lakes, -	Fig. No. 2, Do.
Do. Do., Altered at the Summit, in order to obtain the whole supply of the District,	32	230	178	43 or 60 ft.	5.60	19	4,400, including 260 acres of Lakes.	Fig. No. 3 & 4, Do.
THE BALLINAMUCK LINE, {Canal, - 23¼ / River & Lake, 14}	37¼	191	103	32 6	4.00	11	Not ascertained, but believed to be insufficient.	Fig. No. 5, Do.

March 11th, 1839.   W. T. MULVANY.

Details of the Navigation Possibilities considered by William Mulvany

flood waters. By the end of 1850 three of the river locks had been almost completed while materials had been prepared for building three more. By then, too, the masonry of half of the remaining eight locks, on the still-water section west of Lough Scur, had been completed and progress was very advanced on the rest. The average estimated cost of the locks was £1,500, of which £1,300 was for masonry. The building of the lock gates began late in 1850, much of the work being done at Belturbet, but the locks were not nearly ready for use by the end of 1852; indeed, Skelan [Kiltynaskellan] lock had not even been started. Likewise, several years were to elapse before the weirs were completed.

One task which was finished early on, however, was the construction of three wharves along the canal. By late 1850 the wharves at Ballyconnell, Ballinamore and Leitrim had been completed, and another work very well advanced was the diversion of 'the course of the mountain streams into the lakes which lie along the line of the navigation'. The need for the latter was later explained:

It was also considered necessary in order to keep the canal free from interruption as far as practicable after completion that the courses of the

Yellow and Aghacashlaun Rivers should be diverted by new lines of discharge into St John's Lake and Lough Scur respectively, at the point where they approach these lakes thereby providing for the throwing down and depositing of the large quantities of sand and gravel with which they are charged in time of floods at places where neither the navigation nor the drainage would be injuriously affected.

In fact, two rivers were diverted into Lough Scur — the Kiltubrid [Driny] River which was channelled through a new rock cut to the western side of the lake, and the Aghacashlaun River which formerly flowed down to Castlefore and thence eastwards to St John's Lough at Muckros; the latter river was now diverted westwards into Lough Scur. Both these diversions were essentially complete by the end of 1851 and the same was true of the Yellow River which, instead of flowing south-eastwards to Creevy now swung to the south-west to the northernmost tip of Kiltybardan Lough in the St John's Lough system.

As was the case on very many river navigations the presence of mills posed some tricky problems on the Ballinamore project. While Ballyduff cornmill was by then disused, the opposite was the case with the cornmills at Kilclare and Ballinamore and the corn and flour mills at Ballyconnell. The last-mentioned place was undoubtedly the most important, though there were difficulties over all three locations.

Eel fisheries also caused the odd headache for the OPW. Arrangements were made to purchase the eel weirs on the river at Garadice and Kilnacreevy. There was also an eel fishery at the old weir in Ballyconnell Demesne which was removed early on in the works. In 1851 a plan was produced for regulating sluices and an eel fishery in the demesne and the work was virtually completed in 1852.

Progress and Problems

Despite the multitude of topics which had to be dealt with, the work — while very protracted and continually beset by a lack of funds — was not subject to all that much difficulty. Accidents to men were few and disputes not too numerous, either involving the labourers or connected with the entry to and occupation of lands. Undoubtedly the biggest threat to the proceedings was the financial position, for as time went on it became clear that, for whatever reason, the estimates were hopelessly wrong. By the end of 1852, when the works were nowhere near completion, the expenditure was £173,969 — a far cry from the estimated £131,858! It was reckoned then that £19,007 would be enough to complete the work, but time was to show that proportionately this was an even more erroneous assessment of the situation.

The position did not improve until the passing on 14 August 1855 of an Act which permitted the 'Application of certain Sums granted by Parliament for Drainage and other Works of public Utility in Ireland, towards the Completion of certain Navigations undertaken in connection with Drainages'. Thus the chances of the Ballinamore project being completed improved considerably. The Treasury was empowered to cause alterations or curtailments of the schemes to be made and it could also reduce the portion of the cost to be charged on the counties concerned, any such amounts remitted to be considered as free grants. This was to benefit the district greatly. The Act also allowed the OPW to transfer, with Treasury consent, the completed navigations to the counties as their public property; previous Acts had stipulated that the OPW should retain control of the working navigations.

By the time of this Act, however, the OPW had already been compelled to take some drastic economy measures. At a meeting held on 13 November 1854 the OPW ordered that:

> All the portions of the main channel for the navigation which have not already been completed to a greater depth than 4ft6in [1.35m] below the proposed level of summer water in the reach are now to be dredged or excavated to that depth only — that is, to within 18 inches [0.45m] of the bottom level originally intended in all the reaches except that between Skelan and Aghoo Locks, and that between Ballyduff and Castlefore Locks, in which two reaches it has already been decided to raise the level of summer water 1 foot [0.3m] and to deepen the channel to within 2ft6in [0.75m] of the bottom level originally intended.

The reason for this latter change was the difficulty which Mulvany, the engineer, had been experiencing with the channel excavation in those reaches. Serious slipping of the banks had occurred and even to attain the reduced depth Mulvany thought that dredging would be necessary 'as there is much less likelihood of the bottom rising when the water is in the channel than when it is attempted to carry on the sinking by means of excavation within dams'.

The OPW ordered that the masonry of the locks and weirs concerned be 'carried out to suit the levels for which they were designed without any alteration' and this meant that the proposed raising of the summer level by a foot had to be effected by placing boards on the crests of the weirs at Skelan and Ballyduff. On the other hand, a few months previously the OPW authorised extra works on the new cuts for the Yellow and Aghacashlaun river diversions which would feed the navigation, so not all its moves were negative.

Meanwhile, work was continuing, even if at times fitfully, along the length of the navigation. Labour still proved difficult to obtain and the numbers of men at work fell steadily. In 1854 there was a mammoth effort to clear a difficult stretch, advantage being taken of the stoppage of Ballyconnell mills for some repairs:

> The river at Skelan was completely closed by a dam, which had the effect of ponding up the water in Garadice Lake and the other lakes on the same level. By these means the reach of rivercourse between Ballyconnell and Skelan, about 5 miles [8km] in length, was run dry, or nearly so, and as many labourers as could be got at the time were set to remove any dams, unfinished

portions of shoals, or deposit from the navigation and were so employed until the works at the mill were completed.

Another steam dredger came in mid-1855. Dredger 'C' from the Shannon Navigation was sent to work in the Ballinamore district and by the second week of June it was ready for work, making its way from Leitrim up to Castlefore. A year later 'C' was recorded as having reached Belturbet from Leitrim on 5 August — the first vessel of any size to go right along the navigation. Much dredging was necessary especially at places where slipping of the banks — and hence 'rising of the bottom' had occurred. This trouble was to recur and more or less constant dredging was the only remedy for the problem and also in dealing with the deposition of silt and gravel particularly at the openings into the lakes, notably Garadice.

In 1856 the OPW referred ominously to the 'probable very limited amount of navigation', although Martin Farrell, who had succeeded Mulvany as engineer in charge, reported next year that 'the prospects of the value of the navigation to the country are becoming more apparent as the probability of opening it shortly becomes more generally known'. It was now thought that in autumn 1857 the canal would be 'finally opened for traffic to the public'.

Among the matters still to be tidied up was the provision of a tow-path. Although the brief to McMahon in 1844 had specified a navigation suitable for steamers and, indeed, the presence of the lakes made some sort of independent propulsion essential for boats, the OPW showed a curious insistence on having a tow-path where practicable. In effect this meant that a tow-path, fenced off from the adjoining lands, was made for most but not all of the way from Leitrim to Garadice Lough. In time most of it was gravelled and provided with bridges over streams and drains and, in an early burst of enthusiasm, a tow-path arch was even provided in Ballyconnell Bridge. Just east of Leitrim was a swampy region where there had been a small lake and in 1857 it was reported that 'the tow-path has been formed across the Black Lough, and a covering of cross spars resting on split sleepers has been put on it'.

Another task was the marking of 'the sailing course through certain lakes' and Farrell was told in 1856 that he would need 400 poles, many of which, of larch, were later delivered at Skelan and Aghoo. By 1857 'beacons' had been placed in the lakes and a year later Farrell stated that additional ones had been put up in Coologe, Derrycassan, Ballymagauran and Garadice lakes, and also in St John's Lough, 'to mark more particularly the course from one lake to another'. The OPW drew the line at anything not strictly necessary, however, and in 1858 told Farrell that his proposed 'wickerwork jetties at Garadice Lake' could not be approved, just as it had refused a request for a wharf at Ballinacur two years earlier.

Above: Boats alongside the new mooring at Leitrim.
The Service Block is just visible on the left.

Below: A peaceful setting — Lough Scur in the evening sun.
Note the ancient monument in the foreground.

Above: Tirmactiernan Lock [No 15], viewed from the west,
showing the overflow channel on the right and new access mooring on the left.

Below: Drumduff Lock [No 14], looking eastwards. The overflow weir is in mid-picture.
Also prominent is the traffic light for approaching boats.

Above: Kilclare Lower Lock [No 11], looking towards the next lock [No 10] and bridge [No 7]. Visible over the black control housing is the Waterway Control Centre building at Kilclare Middle Lock [Drumruekill].

Below: View eastwards along the widened Letterfine Rock Cut.

Above: A fine aerial view of the weir, river channel, navigation channel and lock at Castlefore, taken during construction.

Below left: Ardrum Lock [No 5], showing construction detail. In the foreground is the conduit for water, around the upper gates, to fill the lock. Also visible is the cladding with original masonry of the new lock walls. In the background are the weir works and supports for the walkway across the river channel.

Below right: View of Kilclare Middle [No 10; foreground] and Lower [No 11; background] Locks. The lined canal section is visible between the locks. Note the new mooring on the left.

Above: Construction in progress at Castlefore Lock [No 8]. View taken from bridge over east end of the lock.

Left: Detail of lock furniture — the bottom fittings for the heel posts of the gates.

Below: Detail of lock construction — steel reinforcement in place for the wing wall.

Above: Spoil removal and spreading — a view from a workboat.

A tug brings a barge laden with spoil from an ecologically sensitive area to a carefully chosen disposal site.

Below: Pioneering trip — the *Tara Druid* enters the new lock at Corraquill [No 1].

Above: Construction complete — the new weir and walkway at Ballyduff Lock [No 7].

Left: The new fish pass at Ballyduff.

Below: The old footbridge at Rossy.

Further Legislation

The finishing of these smaller but none the less important matters was paralleled by other activity at board and parliamentary level. The 1855 Act had allowed for the handover of the completed works to the public ownership of the four counties concerned, and the procedure to be followed was spelt out even more clearly by an Act which was one of the most important of all — 19 & 20 Vic, c 62, enacted on 21 July 1856. According to its provisions the OPW would decide which were navigation and which were drainage works and the latter would be described in an award and be henceforth given over to locally appointed drainage trustees who would maintain them, funding their efforts by a rate levied off the lands improved by the works. This was the basic procedure for all drainage districts. Thus for well over a century fifteen trustees of the Ballinamore & Ballyconnell Drainage District were chosen by the proprietors at the triennial elections, and every year a programme of drainage maintenance works was carried out.

Under the 1856 Act the navigation works would also be formally described in an award of the OPW, and from the date of the award would:

> vest in the Trustees for the Time being incorporated under this Act for such Navigation, for the use of the Counties, Baronies and Townlands chargeable under such Award, and shall be held, maintained, and preserved by such Trustees.

Navigation trustees were a body corporate 'with perpetual succession and a common seal' and they were quite independent of drainage trustees — an arrangement which was to prove highly anomalous at times. The trustees representing a county could be removed by the appropriate grand jury which had the right to appoint successors.

An equally important purpose of the 1856 Act was to provide for the maintenance of the navigation once the trustees were in control. Section 25 was quite explicit:

> All Expenses of and incident to the Maintenance and Conservancy of [the Navigation] shall (so far as the same may not be defrayed out of the Income aforesaid) be borne and paid by such Counties, Baronies, and Townlands, and Parts thereof respectively, and in such Proportions as by the Award of the said Commissioners of Public Works shall be in this behalf provided.

The procedure was simple enough. The trustees had to send to the grand juries at each spring and summer assizes an account of their receipts and expenditure and they could also send along an estimate of the amount necessary for the expenses of the navigation for the next half-year. The trustees would calculate their probable expenditure, deduct any sums in hand or owing to them, and then pass a demand for the rest to the grand juries, the amount being apportioned among the latter as laid down in the navigation award. Once the counties received the estimate they had to present the

DRAINAGE.

DISTRICT OF

BALLINAMORE AND BALLYCONNELL,

IN THE COUNTIES OF

Cavan, Fermanagh, and Leitrim.

NOTICE is hereby given that the Maps, referred to in the Draft Award for this District, have been lodged at

BALLINAMORE,

IN THE

County of Leitrim,

And all persons interested are at liberty to inspect them on application to the Overseer in charge at that place.

By Order of the Commissioners of Public Works in Ireland,

EDWARD HORNSBY,

Secretary.

Dated at the Office of Public Works,
   Custom House, Dublin,
   this 10th day of November, 1859.

1,812.   250.   12/11, 59.—Printed by ALEX. THOM & SONS, 87, Abbey-street, Dublin.

Nearing the End of the Beginning — One of the last Formal Notices

amounts sought without any choice in the matter; not that in fact they did so without much protest.

This Act was a little premature, as far as the Ballinamore Canal was concerned, for over three years were to pass before the trustees took charge. However, as legally bound to, they held their first meeting on 20 January 1857. Farrell was instructed to attend and to 'afford every information which may be required of you except as regards past expenditure'. Although no known records exist, the trustees were apparently active enough, holding meetings at intervals in spite of the fact that they had as yet no canal to look after. In July 1858 they sought a meeting with Farrell to discuss their fears about the state of the works. He referred the request to Dublin and was quickly briefed:

> There can be no objection to your informing the Trustees of the Ballinamore District of the present condition of the works; but it is clearly out of the question that you should supply a critical statement — pointing out defects &c — which, it is apprehended, is what is required. You may inform the Trustees that upon the District being handed over to them a detailed description of the works, with plans, will be given to them.

The First Boats

Meanwhile the waterway saw the first of the small number of boats ever to use it. There is little concrete evidence about the trade boats using the canal, although there are records of permission to bring boats along it being granted to various people. In December 1856 the lock house contractor was granted permission to use a boat, and, a little later the Ulster Canal Carrying Company's agent at Belturbet, was told that there was no objection to the 'trial trips proposed to be made at Ballyconnell'.

In August 1857 Patrick Buchan, the tenant of the Creevelea ironworks and of coal-pits in the Arigna region, was told he could 'pass a barge laden with coal through the junction canal'. A year later a Mr O'Donovan was likewise approved 'for the conveyance of timber from Ballyconnell to Belfast, provided he undertakes to defray any expense which may be incurred in working the lock [Corraquill] and that he does not attempt to work it without having given due notice in order to secure the presence of an officer of the Board'.

According to Farrell there was an official trial on the canal in 1858:

> In June, a trade-boat was hired from the Ulster Canal, and a load of tiles was brought from Florencecourt tilery to Ballyduff, near Ballinamore. After the delivery of the tiles a load of gravel was taken in at Ballyduff, which was brought to Leitrim. The boat was then taken to Lough Allen, and got a load of coals, which was brought to the steam dredger working at Garadice. It was worked by some of the canal ordinary workmen, and, although some heavy weather was encountered in Lough Allen, only four weeks elapsed between their leaving Crom with the tiles, and delivering the boat up to the Ulster Canal Company, including delivery of the tiles, taking in and delivering the gravel and coals.

In October 1858 James Butler Pratt, the Leitrim county surveyor and later secretary to the trustees, was given clearance to bring a screw steamer on to the canal. Although quite detailed arrangements were made for working through the locks, there is no certainty that a trip was made at that time. However, there were definitely some trade boats on the canal around this period. Farrell stated that in December 1858:

> a double turn in the canal, a little below Ballyconnell, was made wider, to prevent accident to the fan of the screw steamer which, with the Board's permission, had been running between Carrick-on-Shannon and Belturbet since the previous month.

This evidently continued for some time, for next April Farrell was told to report on 'the working of the Junction Canal by the Shannon Steam Navigation Company'. The Ulster Canal Carrying Company — or its successor the Dundalk Steam Navigation Company — also had a boat penetrate at least as far as Ballinamore, carrying 'a good deal of bread stuff'. The vessel in question, a 'steam lighter' with twin bow screws, was the TSS *Shamrock*, formerly owned by William Dargan. A steam yacht launched in mid-1858 by Denny of Dumbarton for the Earl of Erne also made its way along the canal to the Erne, although there is no formal record of its passage. Evidently other boats used the canal as well, for a request was made in April 1860 for permission 'to raise all the sluices at Skelan Lock to reduce the water' to allow a Mr Close 'to raise the boat, No 30, sunk in the canal'. However, the presence of even a few boats was sure evidence that the waterway was virtually complete and that the district was ready for handover to the trustees.

The Final Formalities

The OPW had to make an award as soon as the navigation 'shall have been completed in such Manner and to such Extent as shall be directed or approved of by the Commissioners of Her Majesty's Treasury'. Such an award would specify the costs of the works and the portion which would be charged on the carefully defined district; it would also set out the mode of repayment of this sum. For the drainage district the OPW would follow a similar procedure.

The Treasury, which would instruct the OPW on the financial aspects of the award, was also interested in the district and its Commissioners of Special Inquiry were investigating the works by February 1859. Their report was signed on 15 July 1859 and it showed that the expenditure up to the previous 25 June had been: *Drainage £48,340 / Navigation £224,460 / Mill Power £1,472* making a total of £274,272 which represented an excess of £140,942 over the original estimate. The inquiry commissioners recommended that the landowners whose property was improved by the drainage works, although liable to pay £27,110, should pay the slightly reduced sum of £25,500 in instalments

One of the old Cavan/Leitrim railway bridges, removed in 1992.

with interest at 4% per annum. About the navigation, the report continued:

> the proportion of the expenditure for which the district set forth in the declaration is legally responsible amounts to one half. The prospects of advantage, however, and of a remunerative return which the project was originally considered to hold out, have, we believe, been materially interfered with and lessened by the altered circumstances of the country at large and the general extension of railways. That mode of conveyance has not yet, however, been brought immediately within reach of the district in question, and we believe that the actual benefit which the district may still derive from the junction canal under energetic management would justify us in recommending that the moiety of the original estimate, viz £49,625, should be required to be repaid, but considering that a portion of the canal has not been completed to the full depth and that a sum of £5,000 would probably yet be required to do so, and looking to the limited extent of the district made liable, and the amount of the rate which will be required to be levied in repayment, we have to submit that the charge should be limited to £30,000, and that the Commissioners of Public Works be accordingly authorised by their Lordships, under the provisions of the Act 18 & 19 Vic, c 110, to prepare an award for that amount, and as we are advised that no interest is legally chargeable in consequence of deferred payment, we have further to recommend that the period for such repayment be limited to five years.

The inquiry commissioners' comments on railway development were valid enough in that the spread of railways very much reduced the need for a Limerick-Belfast navigation, as had been envisaged, but the usefulness of the canal for local trade would not be affected at all. Nonetheless, their remarks have been widely misquoted, the impression being given that direct railway competition killed the canal. The final recommendations of the commissioners concerned the mill at Ballyconnell; it was suggested that a charge of £750 be made on the proprietor and included in the drainage award.

On 10 January 1860, two OPW members signed and sealed the final award for the Navigation District of Ballinamore and Ballyconnell, and the navigation was vested in the trustees appointed nearly four years earlier. The financial details were clearly set out — the navigation works had cost £228,651 10s 5d [£228,651.52] inclusive of interest, of which all but £30,000 would be deemed a free grant. The £30,000 was to be repaid by ten half-yearly instalments, the respective county burdens being:

County	Total charged		Proportion of whole
Cavan	£10,029 12s	[£10,029.60]	0.33432
Fermanagh	£ 2,550 18s	[£ 2,550.90]	0.08503
Leitrim	£12,720 6s	[£12,720.30]	0.42401
Roscommon	£ 4,699 4s	[£ 4,699.20]	0.15664
	———		———
	£30,000		1.00000

The proportions were very important, for the award confirmed that future levies for maintenance would be apportioned in exactly the same way on a specified list of townlands which were set out in a very lengthy appendix. A second schedule listed the works which were to be maintained 'as works of Navigation' by the navigation trustees.

The drainage award was not settled on this occasion, however, as some objections to valuations were upheld. The OPW recommended to the Treasury that the £25,500 charge suggested by the inquiry commissioners be reduced to £24,412 and it was this sum which was ordered to be charged over 22 years with interest at 4 per cent by the 'Drainage & Water Power' award which was signed and made final on 6 March 1860. This award confirmed the Ballyconnell mill charge as £750, to be repaid in like manner.

Once the awards were made final there were relatively few formalities left. In February 1860 the OPW asked the Treasury to sanction formally the issue of the necessary warrant by which the transfer of the navigation to the trustees would be made. On 16 March the secretary of each of the four grand juries was sent a copy of the warrant

> directing that the Ballinamore & Ballyconnell Navigation with the tolls thereof shall become the public property of the counties in which the lands chargeable under the Award of the Commissioners [of Public Works] are respectively situate.

The OPW wrote to the trustees on 28 April asking that they appoint someone to receive 'the maps and plans, keys of the collectors' and lock-keepers' houses, and such portions of the moveable gearing in connection with the locks &c...' and on 4 July 1860, after various delays, the navigation finally passed to the navigation trustees.

DRAINAGE.

Acts 5 & 6 Vic., Cap. 89; 8 & 9 Vic., Cap. 69; 9 Vic., Cap. 4; 10 & 11 Vic., Cap. 79; 16 & 17 Vic., Cap. 130; 18 & 19 Vic., Cap. 110; and 19 & 20 Vic., Cap. 62.

DISTRICT OF
BALLINAMORE AND BALLYCONNELL,
IN THE COUNTIES OF
CAVAN, FERMANAGH, AND LEITRIM.

Meeting to appoint Trustees.

We, the Commissioners of Public Works in Ireland, acting in execution of an Act made and passed in the 5th & 6th years of the reign of Her present Majesty Queen Victoria, intituled "An Act to promote the Drainage of Lands and Improvement of Navigation and Water-power in connexion with such Drainage in Ireland," and the several Acts since passed amending the same, hereby call a MEETING of the Proprietors of the Lands included in the

BALLINAMORE AND BALLYCONNELL DISTRICT,

In order to make choice of Trustees, not exceeding Fifteen in number, in the manner directed by and pursuant to the provisions of said Acts, or some or one of them. And Notice is hereby further given, that *such Meeting will be held at the*

COURT HOUSE, BALLYCONNELL,

On Tuesday, the 15th day of May next,

At the hour of One o'clock in the Afternoon of said day, of which all parties concerned are required to take Notice.

R. GRIFFITH,
J. G. M'KERLIE, } *Two of the Commissioners of Public Works in Ireland.*

Dated at the Office of Public Works,
Custom House, Dublin,
22nd March, 1860.

2,977. 500. 23/3, 60. Printed by ALEX. THOM & SONS, 87, Abbey-street, Dublin.

The First Appointments of Drainage Trustees are announced.

19 & 20 VICTORIÆ, CHAP. 62.

BALLINAMORE AND BALLYCONNELL NAVIGATION.

BYE-LAWS

AND

REGULATIONS

MADE

BY THE TRUSTEES

OF THE

BALLINAMORE AND BALLYCONNELL

NAVIGATION,

FOR

MAINTAINING THE WORKS, AND CONDUCTING THE TRAFFIC OF THIS NAVIGATION.

March, 1862.

Trustees:

F. J. BRENNAN, Printer, Carrick-on-Shannon.

The Title Page of the Navigation By-Laws and Regulations [courtesy Mr J.Carty, OPW]

On the waterway after reconstruction, in April 1994. Photos: Frank Miller, The Irish Times

BALLINAMORE AND BALLYCONNELL NAVIGATION.

Act 19th and 20th Vict., Chap. 62.

BYE LAWS.

WE, the TRUSTEES of the Ballinamore and Ballyconnell Navigation District, in pursuance of the Act 19 and 20 Vict., chap. 62, entitled, "An Act to provide for the Maintenance of Navigation made in connexion with Drainage, and to make further provisions in relation to Works of Drainage in Ireland," do hereby make the following Bye-Laws:

I.—Any person who shall force, or attempt to force, any Vessel or Raft through or upon any part of the said Navigation, contrary to these Bye-Laws, or who shall attempt to rescue or take back any Vessel or Raft seized for Tolls or Dues, shall, for every such offence, pay a Fine not exceeding £5, nor less than £2.

II.—No Vessel or Raft shall use or be allowed to ply on any part of this Navigation, whose length shall exceed 80 feet, or whose width shall exceed 15 feet.

III.—The Name of each Vessel and that of her Owner shall be legibly Painted on each side, in Letters, each not less than Six inches long, on Vessels over Ten Tons burden, and not less than 3 inches on Vessels of Ten Tons, or less; and any Master or Owner using or Navigating any Vessel not Painted as aforesaid, shall be liable to a Fine of 5s. for every day such offence shall have continued.

IV.—The Stem and Stern of each Vessel plying on this Navigation, shall be duly graduated, and legibly marked in feet and inches, in a perpendicular line, commencing at lowest edge of Keel and terminating Six inches above deepest Water-line ; and shall be Registered, at some one of the Stations, in the Schedule hereunto annexed mentioned ; and any Master or Owner using or Navigating such Vessel, not so truly and legibly graduated and marked, and not so Registered as aforesaid, shall be liable to pay a Fine of 5s. for every day such offence shall have continued.

V.—The Engineers, Superintendants, and Lock-keepers of the Trustees are hereby empowered to Guage all Vessels using this Navigation, and to deliver to the Owner or Master a Table of such Guaging or Tonnage ; and any Master or Owner refusing to produce or exhibit such Table of Guaging or Tonnage, when so required by any such Engineer, Superintendant or Lock-keeper of the Trustees, shall, for every such offence, pay a Fine not exceeding £5, nor less than £1.

VI.—Any Vessel drawing more than Four feet of Water, shall not ply on, or be allowed to use, this Navigation, or any part thereof.

VII.—The Master or Owner of each Vessel plying on, or using, this Navigation, shall be provided with a Pass or Permit, acknowledging the receipt of all Monies, Tolls, and Rates, paid in respect of same, and Signed and Certified by the Lock-keepers at the several Stations through which the Vessel shall have passed.

VIII.—The Master or Owner of each Vessel shall produce, when so required by any Engineer or Lock-keeper of the Trustees, his Pass or Permit, and a true Manifest or Statement of the Description and Weight of the Cargo ; and any Master or Owner who shall refuse or fail to produce for inspection, when so required, such Manifest or Description, or such Pass or Permit, shall pay a Fine not exceeding £5, nor less than £1 ; and no Vessel shall be allowed to proceed until such Manifest shall have been properly made out, and delivered for inspection of the Lock-keeper or Engineer ; and all Monies, Tolls, and Rates, payable by such Vessel duly discharged.

An Extract from the By-Laws of 1862 [courtesy Mr J. Carty, OPW]

CHAPTER 3

THE LONG DECLINE

On 4 July 1860 J.B. Pratt took charge of the canal from the OPW and on the same day he submitted a report on its condition to the trustees and made application to the OPW for a loan of £800 for two years' maintenance. The OPW acknowledged the report without comment and pointed out that under 19 & 20 Vic, c 62 he should ask the Treasury for a loan of £500 for one year's maintenance. This he did, and at the beginning of August the desired advance was made by the Treasury on the recommendation of the OPW.

Letters flowed from the OPW to Pratt, one stating that the OPW had sold hay along the banks for several seasons past and recommending that the trustees should continue the practice, it being 'very desirable' that it should be done 'for the sake of preventing parties establishing claims by rights of usage', and another, referring to the trustees' suggestion that suitable mill sites might be let, and stating bluntly (and correctly, according to the Acts):

> No water power or mill site in connection with the navigation [is] vested in the trustees and they have therefore no power of making any such letting as referred to.

This did not impress the trustees, who ignored the statement and placed a series of newspaper advertisements which proclaimed the opening of the canal, offered to lease the tolls (unsuccessfully), and announced the intention to lease the 'water power and several mill sites' on the canal (almost equally unsuccessfully). In time, Pat Doherty of Kilclare made a deal with the trustees and for £5 a year won the 'right' to take water for his mill from the canal. In all the trustees got £48 from the Kilclare miller — a sum which when supplemented by the rental of the spoil banks along the canal (the trustees took the OPW advice on this point!) far exceeded the amount ever received in tolls.

Tradition, apparently based on a statement by OPW engineer Robert Manning in 1881, holds that only 8 boats ever used the canal while it was officially open. This is definitely an underestimation, as there are indications that tolls were paid on eight occasions giving a grand total of something over £18 as the maximum sum received for traffic on a navigation costing almost £¼ million! This was in the period 1862-7, outside which other boats are known to have passed, apparently toll-free. Pratt claimed years later that he had brought a boatload of coal from Arigna to Enniskillen, using a borrowed steamer, but this may have been before 1860 and not in 1861 as he recalled.

In 1868 the SS *Knockninny*, built in Dublin for the Erne, was taken along the canal; she was owned by J.G.V. Porter, a son of one of the trustees, and possibly on this account no tolls were charged. By the time the last boat passed, by 1873 at the latest, the trustees had lost interest in tolls. This last vessel was W.R. Potts's carvel-built yacht *Audax* which went from the Erne to the Shannon. But whatever the precise number of boats it seems certain that the total for the years from 1860 onwards cannot have exceeded a pathetic fifteen.

One thorny question first arose in January 1861 and it was to recur many times — the maintenance of the wooden accommodation bridges over the navigation. It was referred by Pratt to the OPW which replied that it 'would refer them to the Navigation Award...as to the bridges to be maintained'. This was a neat evasion of the issue, as a study of the drainage and navigation awards — separate documents which should have been independent — leads to the conclusion that the navigation award, prepared first, was drawn up in a hurry and that the OPW belatedly realized this and tried to tie up any loose ends in the later drainage award. Certainly the navigation works are defined much more fully in the drainage award which also revealed that the maintenance of the accommodation bridges across the navigation channel was the responsibility of the drainage trustees! Generally, both bodies of trustees took the line that if a feature needing repair was mentioned in their award they would undertake the job, otherwise not. The loose terminology of the award schedules which set out the works did not help matters at all.

James Butler Pratt Reports

Notwithstanding all the correspondence there was one major topic on which the OPW was amazingly silent — the condition of the navigation. While Pratt had indicated right at the outset that its condition was, to say the least, rather less than perfect, he was not aware just how bad the position was. The trustees had made a serious error in not commissioning long before they took control the survey which Pratt made in autumn 1860. He made a detailed report in October and it was a fascinating document. It first described the canal, noting that the summit level was 79ft [24m] above the Shannon at Leitrim [reached through 8 locks with an average lift of 9ft10.5in (3m)], and 66ft [20m] above the level of the Erne [each of the other 8 locks having an average lift of 8ft3.5in (2.5m)]. It then turned to the depth of water which was originally intended to be 6ft [1.8m]:

> The works have been executed for a depth of only four and a half feet [1.35m],

BALLINAMORE AND BALLYCONNELL NAVIGATION.

19 & 20 *Victoriæ, Chap. 62, Sec. 15.*

Tolls Chargeable at per Ton, per Mile, on *Ballinamore* and *Ballyconnell Navigation*, for all Vessels and Rafts plying thereon.

1st CLASS Goods, at a ½d. per ton, per mile :

Butter,	Fish,
Tea and Groceries,	Steel and Lead,
Earthenware,	Leather,
Haberdashery,	Linen and Soft Goods,
Hardware,	Spirits.

2nd CLASS, at a ¼d. per ton, per mile :

Tiles & Brick—Sand & Gravel,	Slates and Roofing Tiles,
Pork, Beef, Cattle, and Pigs,	Iron, Steel, and other Metal,
Limestone and other Stone,	Timber and Rafts,
Grain, Potatoes, Meal, & Flour,	Coals and Turf,
Salt and Chemicals,	Guano and Artificial Manures.

SPECIAL CLASS.—HAY, STRAW, MANURE.

All Vessels over 5 Tons, using the Lakes, and not passing through Locks, to pay £1 a Year; and any loaded Vessel passing through a Lock from a point intermediate between any two Stations, shall be charged the Mileage rate per ton, as if she started from the next Station; but all empty Vessels shall be charged 6d. for each Lock passed. Pleasure and Rowing Boats using the Lakes, to pay 2s. 6d. a Year, and to be charged 6d. for each Lock passed.

WHARFAGE.

ARTICLES AND GOODS NAMED.—*First Class,* to pay a 1d. per ton Wharfage, and to be removed within 24 hours; and if not removed in 24 hours, to be charged 1d. per Ton, each day after.

ARTICLES AND GOODS.—*Second Class,* to pay ½d. per Ton Wharfage, and to be removed within 24 hours; and if not removed within 24 hours, to be charged ½d. per Ton, per day.

TABLE OF STATIONS, AND DISTANCES, AND RATES.

FROM.	TO.	MILES.	Total Distance from Shannon.	RATES. 1st Class. ½d. a Mile, per Ton. s. D.	RATES. 2nd Class. ¼d. a Mile, per Ton. s. D.
			MILES.		
The Shannon at Leitrim,	Castlefore Lock,	8	8	0 4	0 2
Castlefore Lock,	Ballyduff Lock,	4	12	0 6	0 3
Ballyduff Lock,	Ballinamore,	2	14	0 7	0 3½
Ballinamore,	Aughoo,	2½	18½	0 9½	0 4½
Aughoo,	Ballinacor Bridge, (Newtowngore,)	3½	22	0 11	0 5½
Ballinacor Bridge, (Newtowngore,)	Skelan Lock,	3	25	1 0½	0 6½
Skelan Lock,	Ballyconnell,	5	30	1 3	0 7½
Ballyconnell,	Carroul Lock,	4	34	1 5	0 8½
Carroul Lock,	Lough Erne,	5	39	1 7½	0 9½

By Order of Trustees,

J. B. PRATT,
Engineer and Secretary.

Official Notice of the Tolls on the Navigation [courtesy Mr J. Carty, OPW]

and this depth...has not been carried out, as there are parts of the navigation
not more than three and a half feet [1.05m] deep, unless when the water is
kept up by putting a board on the weir walls. The water in the lakes between
Castlefore and Ballyconnell is kept about two feet [0.6m] higher than the
level proposed by Mr McMahon in his original report and plans, and this is
done in order to keep four and a half feet [1.05m] of water on the shallows
of these lakes, which shallows...were to be removed. When there are six feet
[1.8m] of water on the lock of Castlefore, the shallows in Lough Scur, the
summit level, vary, from four to five feet [1.2-1.5m], and in dry weather, in
summer, the supply to the summit level is not sufficient to maintain the water
at this height, the leakage through the lock and weir at Castlefore and
through the banks and lock No 9, at Kilclare, reduce the water about sixteen
inches [0.4m].

This was perhaps the most serious complaint but the thorough Pratt continued with a catalogue of other defects — the banks were too steeply sloped
and were giving way 'and have caused a deposit of mud in some places two
feet [0.6m] deep'; the fencing was 'entirely defective'; the tow-path was badly
made; some of the locks were ill-made and most of them leaked considerably
'through the joints of the masonry'. The locks at Skelan, Castlefore and
Kilclare, in particular, were very bad. Indeed, at Kilclare 'the leakage through
the bank and lock No 9 is so considerable that the waste water is sufficient to
turn Kilclare Mill the whole year'. The lock houses were built of 'badly burnt
and unsound brick' and were 'crumbling down with the weather'.

The 'approaches to most of the bridges, as at Newbrook, Kilclare and
Aghoo' had subsided while all the wooden bridges were badly made and 'not
safe for traffic'. The old bridge at Derrygoan made of stone had been replaced
by a wooden structure which was now 'in a dangerous state'. Pratt also
commented on the sluices erected at the weirs on the eastern section of the
waterway; they were not self-acting and were 'very troublesome to attend to
in floods. He wound up his list of complaints with a firm statement:

> It is evident, from the foregoing, that traffic cannot be carried on except by
> small steamers, and that the works now necessary to make the navigation
> available, and protect the public, should not come under the head of repairs,
> but as works necessary to open and complete the navigation, as all the works
> now required were wanting before the canal was given over to the trustees.

The report, along with a detailed estimate of the 'expense of finishing and
repairing the several works above referred to, which estimate amounts on the
whole to £1,718', was sent off to the OPW which made only the briefest reply,
its secretary being instructed:

> Inform Mr Pratt that the Board cannot undertake the repairs which it is the
> duty of the trustees to perform at the cost of the district, of which the
> navigation is the property.

Thereupon Pratt's detailed report was pigeon-holed and it was to lie unseen
and unpublished for over 15 years.

The Trustees do their best

And so it was up to the trustees themselves to do something about their unfortunate waterway. While they could have contented themselves with keeping the works in the precise state in which they received them, this would not have improved their chances of earning anything from boats and so they set out to carry out what repairs they could with the £500 borrowed from the Treasury, a sum supplemented by the amounts levied off the counties. However, it was apparent even at this early stage that to obtain money from the counties, Acts notwithstanding, would never be the easiest of procedures. Roscommon was the first to baulk and early in 1860 a memorial was sent to the Treasury praying that:

> the Barony of Boyle in the County of Roscommon may be relieved from the charge imposed on it in respect of the navigation between the Shannon and the Erne.

It was referred to the OPW which made the telling point that the region was specified in the 1847 declaration and continued:

> The first instalment of the charge certified for pursuant to [the Final] Award has also been presented for by the Grand Jury of the county, by or on behalf of whom, or by any person concerned, no representation was made when the opportunity was given, and the Board are advised that their Lordships [of the Treasury] are not now empowered to cancel any part of that Award.

An attempt was made in summer 1860 to block the payment of the sum presented by Roscommon Grand Jury but it proved unsuccessful and the amount was paid along with subsequent ones. The other counties also paid off their share of the capital charge along with the periodic maintenance levies but the trustees had to engage a solicitor to apply pressure at times.

The trustees first tackled the maintenance of the locks. Then they had the fences and bridges attended to. While the work was commencing the advertisement placed by the trustees was meeting with absolutely no response from boat owners, who seemingly avoided the canal completely. For a few years, however, the trustees pressed on with their maintenance but they then began to have doubts, or as Pratt later put it 'they began to think it was no use'. They decided to make a final attempt to attract boats. A second, rather longer advertisement was placed in eleven newspapers even more widely dispersed throughout the country in mid-1864. But again there was no response and from then on thoughts of maintaining the waterway in a fit state for boats began to recede.

However, there was no definite decision to abandon the navigation as such and to concentrate solely on maintenance of the channel and works for drainage purposes only. It has been stated quite authoritatively at times that such a decision was taken in 1865, but repairs to locks — sometimes extensive as at Ballyduff and Skelan in 1867 — were being carried on as late as 1871. In the latter year the first known contract for the clearing of mud and debris from the channel was granted to Charles Gill, the toll collector at Killarcan, and this set the pattern of most later maintenance works.

Notwithstanding this maintenance the condition of the canal was definitely on the decline, as evidenced by the experience of J.G.V. Porter when he brought the *Knockninny* along the canal from the Shannon late in 1868:

> Only through the kindness of the people, and Mr Pratt, the engineer, was I able to get through the canal. They took the greatest trouble to get water from one reach to another to float me down. But my coming through it is no proof [of its navigability] for it took me three weeks to get through.

Decline Sets In

If that was the case in 1868 things must have been very much worse some five years later when the *Audax* made its voyage from Erne to Shannon. One could not blame the trustees for running down and eventually ceasing their maintenance of purely navigation works. The passage of a decade with about a dozen boats had shown beyond question that no one was interested in the link — the growth of railways had apparently taken care of that — while there

The Navigation Trustee's advertisement of 1864

turned out to be no local traffic to warrant the retention of the waterway.

From the early 1870s the navigation was being neglected and it deteriorated seriously. Admittedly, the lock keepers were to continue in office for some years, receiving their meagre wages. But they had little to do and, east of the summit level, their principal task was the regulation of flood waters by proper control of the large weir sluices. Maintenance work was curtailed and effort concentrated on keeping the main channel reasonably clear as a drainage artery. That was the extent to which the trustees would go.

Prompted by a memorial that there be a partial restoration of the canal, OPW engineer Robert Manning examined the canal from Ballinamore westwards, estimating the cost of its restoration at £4,400 in his report of 10 June 1875. The views of the OPW on the matter were:

> As this navigation has never been made use of since handed over to the trustees, representing the counties of Cavan, Leitrim, Fermanagh and Roscommon, through which it passes [sic], and as the outlay of so large a sum as Mr Manning's estimate would impose a heavy charge on the county of Leitrim, the Commissioners think it would be desirable that the views of the trustees should be ascertained before further steps be taken.

The matter was referred to the trustees, passed back with suitably critical comment, and again referred to the OPW which gave its final opinion:

> The prospects of any trade arising on the navigation, or of any benefits to the surrounding districts there from, are not such as would appear to warrant the expenditure estimated at £4,400.

The Sluice at Ballyconnell Weir in 1970

That ended all talk of restoring the waterway and the decline went on uncontrolled, by now uninterrupted by any maintenance activity. For by 1876 the trustees had more or less decided to cease operations. In 1877 most of the lock keepers received their last pay and those still nominally on the pay-roll would not receive any further remuneration for many years. The last rents had been collected from the tenants of the spoil banks some years earlier, and the last trustees' meeting known to have been held at this period took place at the Hibernian Hotel in Dublin on 26 April 1878 when, presumably, they decided to call it a day.

Official Inquiries

But the waterway was not forgotten — not by a long way. Within 3 years it would be discussed at length before two inquiries. First was a Committee of Inquiry into the activities of the OPW, appointed by the Treasury and with Viscount Crichton as its chairman. Some very interesting evidence was given at the hearings in late 1877. One of the first witnesses was the OPW chairman, Colonel J.G. McKerlie, whose main concern was in maintaining that the trustees were fully aware of the condition of the canal before the award had been made final. He pointed out that no objections had been made at that stage.

Some colourful evidence was given by a trustee, the articulate John Grey Vesey Porter of Belleisle. He was mainly concerned about the failure of interested parties to have an inquiry held into the state of the Ballinamore Canal. Fermanagh Grand Jury, which appointed him as a trustee, had at recent assizes passed 'two strong resolutions' seeking a Government inquiry, something which the trustees themselves had unsuccessfully sought in 1875. To Porter the reasons were clear enough:

> Here is a report of the Commissioners of Inquiry in 1859, into this very canal, and what do I find? At page 8 the signatures of Richard Griffith and J.G. McKerlie, Special Commissioners of Inquiry into the Drainage of Ireland; and at page 13 there is a report, signed by the same Richard Griffith and J.G. McKerlie, as Commissioners of Public Works. The same two men sitting at Cavan in one capacity, and pretending to inquire into their own acts, are sitting in Dublin in another capacity. There is a specimen of the manner in which public business is done in Ireland.

On the question of the state of the canal Porter commented that the trustees were wrong in accepting charge from the OPW 'merely on their statement that it was duly finished, and without any competent and independent inquiry'. This omission, he felt, was 'the principal cause of all this trouble'.

Colonel McKerlie was re-examined and he had a shot at rebutting Porter's evidence, but his plaintive claim that 'there was a connection of a navigable character when the works were completed' could hardly have cut much ice with the committee. Its report appeared in 1878 and there were some harsh words about the canal in its pages. Noting that the trustees were 'doubtless very insufficiently aware of the cumbersome charge they were taking over' the report continued:

> The absolutely useless condition of the canal, indeed, was only made clear in the report of Mr Pratt...immediately after the transfer had taken place. That report was duly forwarded to the Board of Works; but the facts disclosed in it, which are tolerably conclusive, have never been made public till now...The Board made no inquiry into the validity of these allegations, but contented themselves with denying their responsibility and refusing to undertake the repairs. There is in consequence no counter official report to show what was at the time the condition of the canal; but if eighteen years ago the works were in the state pointed out by Mr Pratt, and nothing has since been done to improve them, it is no wonder that the canal should now be choked with mud and weeds, and be utterly useless.

On the much discussed wider question of the wisdom of retaining all the 'northern waterways' the committee was unsure and it recommended the setting up of a royal commission to investigate the matter.

The Crichton Committee had its wish for a further inquiry granted. In 1881 a royal commission with Viscount Monck as chairman was appointed to investigate the 'System of Navigation which connects Coleraine, Belfast and Limerick', and of course the Ballinamore Canal featured prominently in the evidence which was heard in mid-1881. Once again the redoubtable J.G.V. Porter testified in his picturesque fashion:

> You see birds sitting on the mud at some places in the middle of the canal. It is wonderful jobbing. That canal is a chapter in Irish history that ought to be better known.

Robert Manning was next to give evidence and he gave details of his 1875 inspection of the western half of the canal. He recounted that all the masonry works were well constructed and in good condition, but that the lock gates were 'completely out of order and gone to decay...rotten, in fact'. While he was in the area he had made inquiries and had been told that only eight boats had used the canal. Manning quoted a letter of March 1876 from the trustees in which they expressed their wish to maintain the works for drainage only 'as there is not, and never has been, any traffic of any kind, nor is there likely to be any traffic to justify keeping the navigation part in repair' but, as has been indicated above, by the late 1870s all maintenance was abandoned.

The report of the Commission, issued in 1882, outlined the history of the canal right from the start and gave details of its condition. It agreed with those who dismissed its utility as a navigable waterway:

> The evidence submitted to us goes to show that the restoration of the navigation would be of little benefit to the public, that there would be no profitable traffic upon it, and further that there would be a great disinclination on the part of the local tax-payers to support it.
>
> The canal has, however, a completely different aspect when viewed as a drainage work. The evidence is unanimous that for drainage purposes it is

most valuable, and that it is of great importance that it should be maintained as an arterial drain.

We recommend that no attempt be made at present to re-establish navigation with public money, and we are of the opinion that the canal should be handed over to trustees, to be preserved and improved as a drainage work only, with this obligation, however, that the banks of the canal, and the masonry of the locks shall be maintained in good repair, so that navigation may be resumed at some future time without incurring any very serious expense, if the circumstances of the country shall require it, the Comm-issioners of Public Works being empowered to execute the necessary works at the expense of the locality on default by the trustees.

Standstill and Revival

The position regarding the Ballinamore Canal in the 1880s is very obscure indeed. No meetings are known to have been held by the trustees between 1878 and 1893, yet there must have been some trustees who took a minimal interest in affairs. J.B. Pratt died on 1 February 1886 and soon afterwards John Joseph Benison took over as acting secretary. But this was largely a nominal post and he did not make any attempt in the 1880s to collect any of the long overdue rents from the spoil bank tenants.

Because of the necessity to maintain a level for the mills it was essential that both the works at the weir and the upper gates at Ballyconnell lock be kept in repair. Thus in 1880 the latter were the only lock gates in order along the whole canal. Soon afterwards they began to deteriorate and by the middle of the decade they were sorely in need of repair. Under the procedure in the Acts a memorial was sent to the OPW which sent an engineer down to investigate. He proposed that a dam be built across the upper end of the lock to keep up the water and a contract was awarded in March 1886 to the miller, William Lang. The work was completed later that year at a cost of £54 which was levied off the surrounding district at the 1887 spring assizes.

By early 1893 the dam and weir at Ballyconnell needed further attention and again a contract for repairs was awarded to William Lang. Apparently the dam needed reconstruction, while there was a leakage at the weir, and the work cost a total of £125, some £20 more than the contract price. The amount was later levied off the district in the usual fashion and the occasion was notable in that it was the last on which the formal procedure from memorial through to ultimate levy on the rate-payers of any drainage district was put into practice according to the drainage Acts.

For reasons now unknown the decision to revive the trustees was taken sometime in 1893. Who took the initiative is also a mystery; it may have been either the grand juries or some of the land owners, both of whom would have been concerned with problems of flooding which would certainly become more serious as the canal channel got ever more choked with silt and decaying vegetation. At any rate, Benison was in contact with Fermanagh Grand Jury

Ballinamore Lock [No 6] in 1970, looking towards Ballyduff

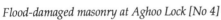

Flood-damaged masonry at Aghoo Lock [No 4]

early in 1894 and some time later an approach was made to the Roscommon jury, both with a view to having new trustees appointed. The moves suggest that it was interested parties in Cavan and Leitrim who started things rolling. Appointment of a permanent secretary was made in 1894 and next year an engineer was chosen. By the time a full board of trustees had been appointed (except of course for Roscommon representatives) it was well into 1895 and the first known regular meeting took place on 28 August.

Maintenance works were not undertaken immediately but a necessary preliminary step was soon made — a levy demand was sent to the counties, three of which paid up promptly. The exception was Roscommon and the trustees had to take proceedings against the grand jury to enforce payment. The matter was not resolved until mid-1898 when a judicial decision given in Dublin ordered that payment be made. By 1899 the trustees were ready to recommence maintenance work and once again the location was Ballyconnell, where the weir sluice needed replacement as, possibly, did the dam at the lock. The work was undertaken in mid-year and cost over £120.

The main obstacle to the trustees' plans was the lack of enthusiasm on the part of the county authorities when it came to paying the maintenance levies. At this period trustees' meetings were becoming more regular although business was still not back to 'normal'. But this was, in fact, quite an important transition period. Under the Local Government Act of 1898 the old grand juries were replaced by county councils as from mid-1899. All the rights and obligations concerning navigations passed to the councils but the change was none the less very significant. The grand jurors were for the most part prominent landowners who tended to be remote from the troubles which stemmed from the canal. It was their tenants who lost their crops or had to make lengthy detours to the markets when bridges collapsed.

The trustees they appointed were of the same caste; indeed, a property qualification laid down by the 1856 Act ensured this. Thus the navigation board was decidedly on the lethargic side. Now under the new arrangement the county councils, composed of democratically elected members, would be sure to include some of the community directly suffering from the vagaries of the canal. In turn, council-appointed trustees could be expected to take a livelier interest in the problems caused by the navigation.

Further Investigations

Others with an interest in the canal included two more august bodies of inquiry. In 1905 a vice-regal commission on arterial drainage in Ireland was appointed and it heard some evidence on the canal in 1906. One of the trustees, S.B. Roe, gave evidence which confirmed that the trustees were then concentrating mainly on keeping the Ballyconnell works. He also commented on the difficulty in getting payment of the levies, though he stated that Leitrim, not

Roscommon, was the culprit:

> We were unfortunately let in for a good deal of law expenses by the County
> Council of Leitrim. They refused to pay their portion of the assessment, and
> we had to go to law with them. That ran away with some money, which we
> in Cavan and the other counties had to pay.

Roe was not exaggerating — in the years previous an inordinate proportion
of the total revenue had gone in legal expenses.

The canal received far greater attention at the 1906 Royal Commission on
Canals and Waterways. This time the report and some appended documents
were of greater interest, although some of the evidence was worthy of note.
Two witnesses thought that the canal would be a great benefit if restored,
while another, Sir Horace Plunkett, although admitting that the drainage
consideration was paramount, felt that the navigation could be restored at
small relative cost.

The report of the commission sketched out as usual the history of the canal
and commented on its management:

> The works were, in 1860, by a device singularly calculated to promote
> inefficient management, transferred to two bodies of trustees, one for
> drainage purposes, both bodies having powers of taxation for maintenance
> purposes.

The members of the commission felt that not enough evidence had been
submitted to justify them in recommending the restoration of the canal, but
they added — as had both the Crichton and Monck inquiries — the opinion
that:

> this canal should be maintained as a drain, and the masonry and other works
> kept in good repair, so that it could be readily converted into a navigable
> waterway if the time should come when it becomes desirable to connect the
> River Shannon with the Northern Canal System and the port of Belfast.

The 'Best' Years

The years 1912-13 were a landmark for the navigation trustees in that a third
of the board was replaced by new men; the new blood would prove very
beneficial. The next quarter-century was to prove relatively the busiest period
in the history of the navigation since the award and the one pity was that the
effort was directed solely towards drainage, all thoughts of navigation having
been abandoned.

A significant feature of the new era was the holding of regular board
meetings. The trustees met on average three times a year, normally in January,
April and July. At their first meeting they would consider the estimates for the
half-year just beginning and study the maintenance programme proposed by
the engineer. In April they would award contracts for the various works and
in July the business would again be largely financial. The different contractors

would have to be paid and there would be the task of drawing up the estimates and making a levy demand for the second half-year.

The normal procedure in preparing the estimates was simple enough. The engineer submitted to the secretary an estimate of the amount which he thought would be needed for the maintenance works planned for the period in question. To this sum the latter added appropriate amounts to cover salaries and other probable expenditure, but he deducted from the total any sums to the credit of the trustees and also the probable income from rents. The net amount left would then be carefully apportioned among the four counties precisely as laid down by the navigation award. The financial statement, along with a full account of expenditure during the past half-year, was then sent to the counties, whose duty it was to meet the levy.

The secretary was responsible for the collection of rent from the tenants. The average yearly rental was small but, despite the effort involved in collecting it, it was useful in helping to keep down the levy demands. The reason for the very uneven distribution of paying tenants was that the lands for letting by the trustees were those which had been purchased for the canal in the 1850s, and these would not have included all, if any, of the original river banks.

In the selection of the maintenance works to be carried out the trustees were guided by their engineer, whose recommendations in turn were based on requests from farmers for specific improvements and on his own observations made on inspection. The engineer, or superintendent as he was more usually known, would also draw up plans, specifications and estimates for the works which would on approval be advertised and let on contract. This policy was by and large very successful, though at times the going was rough enough for the navigation board. Over the years it received a multitude of complaints from aggrieved people along the canal who often suffered severe losses and were driven to seek the aid of a solicitor. But there was no long history of legal action and the trustees were just about able to keep the situation under control. This was no mean achievement, considering that the average of the 26 half-yearly total levy demands made in the period 1913-35 was just under £125.

Maintenance work began in earnest in 1913 and it was appropriate that the first work to be carried out was on the channel itself rather than on some of the works. It had been nearly 40 years since such a work had been undertaken and it was not before time when William Coulston was given the task of cutting and removing 'trees, shrubs, bushes and brambles' between Ballyconnell and Corraquill locks. In 1914 attention was turned to the stretch just west of Garadice Lake and another important work was carried out at Ballyconnell. It was the trustees' intention that their work should be directed towards flood abatement, hence the clearing of the channel, and it was obvious that something would have to be done at Ballyconnell where the weir and its sluice (even when the latter was in working order) were not fully capable of handling heavy floodwater discharges.

A Notice to Contractors of April 1934

The dam across the face of Ballyconnell lock did not help matters in the least and it was agreed early in 1914 that it should be replaced by a large sluice where the upper gates of the lock once were. In the years following, Ballyconnell continued to occupy an excessive amount of the trustees' time. The new sluice needed attention in 1916 and 1917. By 1919 the sluice gates at the weir were very rotten and had to be replaced, the work being done by direct labour.

The topic of maintenance was on the agenda for the January 1924 meeting and a deputation from Fermanagh attended to describe the flooding caused by obstructions at Corraquill lock. Many farmers were thinking of taking legal action, so bad was the position. The trustees were agreed that the work was necessary but they decided not to undertake it until recent levy arrears had been paid by Fermanagh County Council. To spend money levied off the other counties on works in Fermanagh would, it was felt, be unfair. That was the general policy adopted by the trustees. As far as was practical money levied off a county was spent on maintenance in that county. This was fine but the unfortunate Roscommon rate-payers were left with a levy which went towards the administrative costs of works which were of no benefit at all to them.

For rate-payers of the other three counties, however, the works were decidedly useful, especially as many of the contracts now being awarded were for work on the actual channel. Any cleaning work carried out on it was bound to have a beneficial effect on the neighbouring lands, and it also rendered more effective the work of the drainage trustees, who regularly had the lateral drains under their control cleaned. From time to time the scope of the navigation maintenance would be widened to include the replacement or reconstruction of accommodation bridges in need of attention.

But further repairs at the weir sluice in Ballyconnell did nothing to relieve the plight of the farmers who began to think more and more of legal action. Things came to a head in mid-1931 when there was such heavy rain that the people in Boeshill, near Garadice, lost their entire hay crop; in places boats had to be used to rescue cattle. With commendable speed it was agreed to have a new sluice erected, and the work was shortly afterwards put in hand. This was the last effort put in by the trustees on the Ballyconnell sluices which had occupied so much time and work.

The trustees had certainly given Ballyconnell and its problems all the attention they could and it made a refreshing change when, in the mid-1930s, they concerned themselves with Ballinamore. The basin there was in a highly insanitary condition because of sewage discharges and in times of low flow the position was acute. The trustees were asked to deal with the problem and although arguably not their concern they awarded contracts for cleaning work in 1933 and later years. The last such contract was given in September 1935, for the cleaning of the channel from lock No 5 to the basin and of the old river course for a short distance to Stradermot, a total length of about 250 statute perches. The work was duly executed and what distinguishes it is that, although nobody knew it at the time, it was the last maintenance contract of any kind awarded by the trustees of the navigation district.

The Trustees' Final Efforts

By the 1930s the dissatisfaction of the local authorities with the canal reached a peak and the counties were coming to the conclusion that the question should be settled once and for all. The region 'served' by the canal was essentially a depressed area and its local authorities were always seeking the best value possible for the money they levied in rates. In their view there was little if any worthwhile return to be gained from contributing towards the piecemeal and inadequate maintenance of a white elephant of a navigation.

Leitrim County Council, which had 'always resisted the rate' for the upkeep of the canal, took decisive action in 1936 and instituted legal proceedings against the trustees on a number of grounds. The council terminated the appointments of its trustees by resolution in 1936 and in the following year

BALLINAMORE & BALLYCONNELL

NAVIGATION DISTRICT.

NOTICE

TO

CONTRACTORS.

The Trustees of the above District will, at their Meeting to be held in Ballyconnell on the 30th April, 1935, receive and consider TENDERS for the following Works :—

CO. FERMANAGH.

No. 1—Sinking and Widening Bed of Navigation Canal at Caroula. Cost not to exceed £20.

The Work to be carried out in accordance with the Specification prepared by the Superintendent.

Tender Forms and copies of Specification can be had from the Superintendent or from me up to the hour of Meeting.

The lowest or any Tender not necessarily accepted.

By Order,

Patrick Quinn, Secretary.

Peter Edwards, Superintendent.

Killaphort, Garadice P.O.,
Ballinamore,
8th April, 1935.

A typographically interesting Contractors' Notice of 1935

the remaining trustees, representing Cavan and Fermanagh, resigned. There was an unexpected development in 1940 when Fermanagh County Council appointed three new trustees, the only nominal trustees in office for some years. The judge gave his opinion on the action by Leitrim on 30 July 1943 — the case was dismissed on all counts. The decision left the three new Fermanagh trustees as the sole persons in charge of the navigation district. One wonders what was their reaction to being in control of a navigation which for much the greater part of its length lay outside Northern Ireland.

However, in May 1947, both the Leitrim and Cavan councils appointed three new trustees each. While this may have seemed a promising move there was no follow-up in the form of funds, and the position was not hopeful when the board met on 6 February 1948. This time decisive action, in a sense, came from the trustees. Deciding that there was little point in maintaining an anomalous situation, they ceased their activities, though these now consisted merely of meeting irregularly. This was the last meeting in the 91-year life of the Ballinamore and Ballyconnell Navigation Trustees and once the trustees left Ballyconnell on that February afternoon the administration of the canal went into a state of suspended animation, while the waterway itself continued to decay quietly as it had done for so long previously. Shortly after the trustees ceased to function, the bridge over the canal at Derrymacoffin collapsed — the event was something of a symbolic occurrence.

However, the county councils were aware of the problems which the canal could cause and from 1948 onwards they undertook some important work which might well have been beyond the capabilities of the trustees. They repaired or replaced the accommodation bridges as necessary. The drainage trustees carried out their duties on clearing the lateral drains and channels but the main channel, the canal, remained very largely undisturbed, causing occasional great hardship by flooding to the riparian farmers, whose views on the waterway became increasingly jaundiced.

Early Restoration Calls

However, the canal had its protagonists who, from about the mid-1960s, became ever more articulate on its possible restoration as a navigable waterway. Among them was Leitrim County Council which had been keeping an eye on the increasing number of pleasure boats on the Shannon and, indeed, had fostered the growth by undertaking an excellent development of facilities at Carrick-on-Shannon. Another demand for action came in 1969 when the Inland Waterways Association of Ireland, which had established branches at both Ballinamore and Ballyconnell, called for a survey by a competent firm, being supported by the county council.

In 1970 the latter again pressed for a survey by the OPW, which had dismayed some councillors by pointing out that the Erne catchment was the

Top: The Toll Collector's House alongside Killarcan Lock [No 16]
Bottom: The dilapidated Still-Water Canal near Lock No 9 at Kilclare

tenth on the priority list of the arterial drainage programme and also that the Erne as a whole was a very large catchment and presented engineering problems of great complexity. It was furthermore complicated by the problem of the Border, and consequently a complete scheme would take a very long time to develop as far as the work stage.

The arguments did not impress the council one little bit, the county engineer commenting that the OPW engineers were well capable of putting forward proposals for drainage and navigation which did not conflict. And as for the border question, there would surely be no difficulty on that account, for previously representatives of the Northern Ireland tourist board had indicated a willingness to co-operate in and share the cost of a survey of the canal. The general displeasure was succinctly expressed by one speaker: 'Tourism and agriculture are the only apparent solution to development in County Leitrim and we should expect that a Government Department like the Office of Public Works would be pressing forward such a scheme rather than deferring it.'

Although sincere, these sentiments hardly did justice to the OPW, a government agency whose activities, very frequently large-scale and therefore expensive, had necessarily to be prioritised in the light of available funds. As we shall note in Part Two, those priorities were to be altered radically as far as the Ballinamore Canal was concerned.

The Canal Wharf at Ballyconnell, just downstream of the Bridge

PART TWO

THE SHANNON - ERNE
WATERWAY 1994

Many years ago there was a Ballinamore canal...
It was the finest canal that was built in Britain [sic] up to that time.

Major Harry Lefroy, 1923

The then quite substantial remains of Pat Doherty's Corn Mill at Kilclare, in 1970

Ballinamore and Ballyconnell Drainage District

NOTICE TO CONTRACTORS

The Trustees of Ballinamore and Ballyconnell Drainage District will at their adjourned meeting to be held in the Courthouse, Ballinamore, on Saturday, 29th March, 1969, be prepared to consider tenders for the following works, viz.:

COUNTY LEITRIM

No. 22—680 perches of Castleroggy Stream. Cost not to exceed 4/- per perch or £136.

No. 23—250 perches of drain between Kilrush and Aghyowla. Cost not to exceed 3/- per perch or £37 10/-.

No. 24—180 perches of Georges Lough Stream. Cost not to exceed 3/6 per perch or £31 10/-.

No. 25—164 perches of Dromkeen Drain. Cost not to exceed 4/- per perch or £32 16/-.

No. 26—210 perches of Drain between Drumany and Kiltyfannon. Cost not to exceed 3/6 per perch or £36 15/-.

No. 27—390 perches of Corramahon Drain. Cost not to exceed 3/- per perch or £58 14/-.

No. 28—120 perches of Drain from Killyran Little Lough to Glebe Lough. Cost not to exceed 3/- per perch or £18.

No. 29—204 perches of Newtowngore Stream. Cost not to exceed 3/6 per perch or £35 14/-.

No. 30—196 perches of Tullyoscar Drain. Cost not to exceed 3/- per perch or £29 8/-.

No. 31—350 perches of Moher

No. 43—340 perches of Drumcoura Lough Stream. Cost not to exceed 3/6 per perch or £59 10/-.

No. 44—136 perches of drain between Derrinkip and Leaenish. Cost not to exceed 3/- per perch or £20 8/-.

No. 45—380 perches of Kiltubride River from Boundary between Drumadykey and Annadale Lake, including Annadale Branch. Cost not to exceed 4/- per perch or £76.

No. 46—150 perches of Lisconnor Stream. Cost not to exceed 2/- per perch or £15.

No. 47—120 perches of Keshcarrigan Stream. Cost not to exceed 3/6 per perch or £21.

No. 48—184 perches of Drain between Ardrum and Drumraine-Glebe. Cost not to exceed 3/- per perch or £27 12/-.

No. 49—104 perches of Loughawaddy Stream. Cost not to exceed 3/- per perch or £15 12/-.

No. 50—230 perches of Old Yellow River. Cost not to exceed 3/6 per perch or £40 5/-.

No. 51—150 perches of New Cut Yellow River. Cost not to exceed 2/6 per perch or £18 15/-.

No. 52—208 perches of Drain from Kiltyfannon Lough to Canal. Cost not to exceed 3/6 per perch or £36 8/-.

No. 53—96 perches of Carricport Drain. Cost not to exceed 3/6 per perch or £16 16/-.

No. 54—160 perches of Drain through the townland of Glebe. Cost not to exceed 3/6 per perch or £28.

No. 55—176 perches of Aghnahoo Drain. Cost not to exceed 3/6 per perch or £30 16/-.

No. 56—260 perches of Bellana-

Stream from Dumbibe School to end of Old Yellow River. Cost not to exceed 3/6 per perch or £61 5/-.

No. 32—350 perches of Moher Stream from end of Old Yellow River to Canal. Cost not to exceed 3/6 per perch or £61 5/-.

No. 33—184 perches of Drain between Derrinkip and Drumlitten. Cost not to exceed 3/- per perch or £27 12/-.

No. 34—320 perches of New Cut Kiltubride River. Cost not to exceed 3/6 per perch or £56.

No. 35—122 perches of drain between Corrabeagh and Muckross and between Corrabeagh and Derrymacoffin. Cost not to exceed 3/6 per perch or £19 12/-.

No. 36—264 perches of Edentenny Stream. Cost not to exceed 3/6 per perch or £46 4/-.

No. 37—184 perches of Drain between Mough, Ardrum and Aghoo-West. Cost not to exceed 3/- per perch or £27 12/-.

No. 38—88 perches of Drain between Mough and Ardrum. Cost not to exceed 3/- per perch or £13 4/-.

No. 39—340 perches of County Boundary Drain at Glebe. Cost not to exceed 3/- per perch or £51.

No. 40—150 perches of Ardmeenan Drain. Cost not to exceed 3/- per perch or £22 10/-.

No. 41—290 perches of Carrickverril Drain. Cost not to exceed 3/6 per perch or £50 15/-.

No. 42—440 perches of Kiltubride River from New Cut to Boundary between Drumadykey and Annadale. Cost not to exceed 3/6 per perch or £77.

boy Stream. Cost not to exceed 3/6 per perch or £45 10/-.

No. 57—124 perches of County Boundary Drain, Kilnacreevy. Cost not to exceed 3/6 per perch or £21 14/-.

No. 58—53 perches of Dromore Lough Stream. Cost not to exceed 3/6 per perch or £9 5/-.

No. 59—200 perches of Drain from Lisconnor Bridge to Old Mill at Kiltoher. Cost not to exceed 2/- per perch or £20.

No. 60—136 perches of Leamenish Drain. Cost not to exceed 3/6 per perch or £23 16/-.

No. 61—1028 perches of Fohera River. Cost not to exceed 4/- per perch or £205 12/-.

No. 62—116 perches of Drain between Georges Lough and Camagh Lough. Cost not to exceed 6/- per perch or £34 16/-.

No. 63—96 perches of Killaglasheen Drain. Cost not to exceed 3/6 per perch or £16 16/-.

All works to be carried out in strict accordance with the specification prepared by the Superintendent.

The lowest or any tender not necessarily accepted.

Tender forms can be obtained from the Secretary with whom completed tenders should be lodged by 27th March, 1969.

All works must be completed before 30th August, 1969.

(By Order),

JOHN EDWARDS

Secretary & Superintendent
Drainage Office
Bawnboy, Co. Cavan.
27th February, 1969.

Above: Active after a century — the Drainage Trustees advertise in 1969
Below: On the reconstructed waterway in 1994. Photo: Frank Miller, The Irish Times.

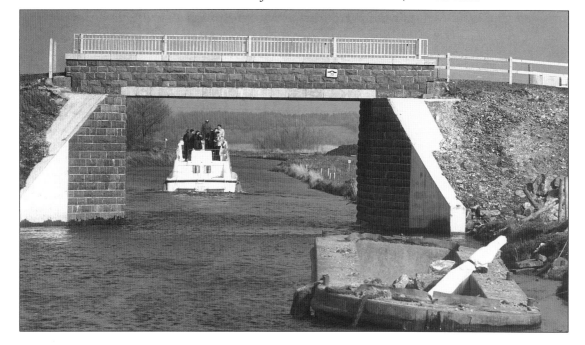

A scenic view along the canal at Kilclare.

Looking west from Bridge No 7, at Kilclare Middle Lock, along the lined section of canal. Note the preserved remnant of Pat Doherty's corn mill on the left.

The weir at Skelan Lock [No 3] with Coologe Bridge [No 25] and Lough in the background. The navigation loops round to the left to reach the bridge.

RINNE AN TAOISEACH, CATHAL Ó HEOCHAIDH, T.D.
AN LEAC CHUIMHNEACHÁIN SEO
A NOCHTADH MAR CHEILIÚRADH AR THOSÚ
AN TIONSCADAIL UM ATHCHÓIRIÚ
CHANÁIL BHÉAL AN ATHA MOIR-BÉAL ATHA CONAILL
DÉ LUAIN, 26 SAMHAIN, 1990
THIS COMMEMORATIVE PLAQUE WAS UNVEILED
BY
THE TAOISEACH MR. CHARLES J. HAUGHEY, T.D.
TO MARK THE LAUNCH OF THE
BALLINAMORE-BALLYCONNELL CANAL RESTORATION PROJECT
ON MONDAY, 26TH NOVEMBER 1990

Above: The Commemorative Stone at Ballinamore Basin.

Left: Above Ballyconnell Lock [No 2] showing the access mooring and short stub leading to the old mill head-race (left). *Right:* The approach to Corraquill Lock [No 1]. The river channel runs to the left foreground.

A placid scene — the basin at Ballinamore showing the commemorative stone.

Above: A new mooring at the Basin in Ballinamore.

Below: The end of navigation — a cruiser turns near the present limit of navigation in Belturbet.

CHAPTER 4

PROPOSALS AND PLANNING

Some 25 years elapsed after the last futile meeting of the Navigation Trustees before there were any major developments in the history of the Ballinamore Canal. For two decades after that 1948 meeting virtually the only voices in support of the restoration of the Shannon-Erne link were those of the members of the Inland Waterways Association of Ireland, who had actively and successfully championed the virtues and benefits of the Shannon navigation itself, and who in 1965 issued a pamphlet in support of the restoration of the Ballinamore and Ballyconnell waterway.

However, by the late 1960s the canal was fairly well in the public eye, at least locally. For a few years past international student work camps had been set up in summer along the canal and much cleaning work had been carried out. In addition, enthusiasts had dredged the basin at Ballinamore. In 1969 local branches of the IWAI held their first boat rally during which a flotilla of small boats had gone from Ballinamore to Ballyconnell. The canal also featured in the programme of events for the annual Ballinamore town festivals, with boat trips being run.

There was a deal of pro-canal publicity which continued into 1971 with occasional letters to the press advocating the restoration as a means of promoting North/South co-operation, and of developing tourism which was seen as the main hope for economic survival in a depressed region. One of a series of articles on Irish waterways in the *Irish Times* called attention to the potential of the canal, drawing a small correspondence in return. But all this was nothing compared to the lead story in the *Irish Press* of 20 May 1971 which proclaimed:

> A link-up between the Rivers Erne and Shannon will be one of the first specific projects to be considered in the new North-South talks on economic co-operation.

The report stated that the Minister for Transport and Power in the Republic had put forward the proposal which was warmly endorsed in the lead editorial. Tourist officials were understandably enthusiastic about the idea.

Questions were asked in parliament a little later on, when it began to emerge that there would be no speedy reopening of the whole canal but rather a more modest start with the restoration of the section from Ballyconnell to the Erne, which would give a waterway link to Belturbet. The Minister stated that an interim survey was being carried out on the stretch below Ballyconnell.

On the question of a reopening west of Ballyconnell the Minister was less specific, noting that 'the drainage of the Woodford Canal, between Ballyconnell, Co Cavan, and Ballinamore, Co Leitrim, was a longterm proposal'. This would be an extension which would depend on a detailed survey. The impression was conveyed that the reopening of the whole canal, however desirable, would not be a step too quickly taken, on the grounds of engineering complexity and overall cost.

There was general agreement among interested parties that what was needed was a thoroughly critical professional survey of the canal and an accurately prepared estimate of the cost of its restoration. The information thus made available would enable all the parties concerned with the canal to come to the best decision. As a first step it was revealed late in 1971 that a 'visual survey' had shown that at least £100,000 would have to be spent to restore navigation to enable cabin cruisers to travel from Lough Erne 'to at least as far as Ballyconnell'.

It was thought that the work would take three summer seasons to complete and that a detailed field survey, made over two months, would be necessary in order to enable firm estimates to be prepared. Given such a full survey setting out the true position along the whole navigation, the governments North and South could consider the matter and, hopefully, give their approval for the reopening.

Although political difficulties at that time disrupted the intended liaison between the governments (and were later to delay consideration of such projects considerably), the Minister for Transport & Power in the South requested the OPW to carry out initially a study of the main works which would be essential if the Ballinamore Canal were to be restored for navigation. This was duly done and after consideration of it the Minister gave approval for a detailed investigation of the feasibility of a restoration and for the necessary engineering studies.

The First OPW Investigation

Most of the actual survey work was carried out in 1972 by engineering staff from the Shannon Navigation section of the OPW, whose personnel undertook much further study and design work over the following decade and after. Drainage implications of any restored navigation had of course to be taken into account, while a primary aim was to arrive at a realistic costing for the works as a whole. As regards drainage, consideration had to be given to the future possibility of a catchment drainage scheme being carried out. In this regard, an important action by the OPW — and one which was to prove invaluable nearly 20 years later — was the establishment in 1973 of a network of hydrometric gauging stations in the Woodford River catchment. One station was established on Lough Scur, five on the main river channel, four on tributary rivers and one on Upper Lough Erne.

Concurrent with these OPW activities was the carrying out of a major tourism and recreational study, commissioned from Brady, Shipman and Martin by Bord Failte (the Irish Tourist board) and the OPW. The remit of this study was specially expanded to take into account the implications of restoring the Ballinamore Canal. The report noted that:

> ......No maintenance work has been done on the canal for a very long period of time, flooding continues to be a major problem and the adjoining local authorities have pressed for the undertaking of a major combined drainage and navigation project which would solve the flood problem and realize the tourism potential which they feel exists in the area. The Office of Public Works has carried out a survey of the waterway but complex engineering studies are necessary to prove the feasibility of such a project.

It continued:

> It is understood that the proposal to reinstate the Ballinamore & Ballyconnell Canal, thus linking the Erne and Shannon Navigations is being examined. Detailed engineering studies are already in hands but the project is unlikely to be realized in the short term. Progress may well depend upon a relaxation of tensions between the north and south. Boating interests are generally in favour of the reopening of the Canal and see it as a major extension to the useful navigation. In practical terms, however, the technical aspects of the problem are formidable and local farming interests will have to be assured that the solution will have a minimal effect on their operations and may help alleviate local flooding problems..... The reopening of the Ballinamore & Ballyconnell Canal in the longer term would seem to be desirable.

That was the position in 1976 and for some years there was little apparent consideration of the Ballinamore canal project. Certainly, the Shannon Navigation section of the OPW was heavily engaged in the upgrading and extension of facilities for pleasure boating on the Shannon itself, where many valuable improvements were made.

But there was still a groundswell of support for the restoration, fuelled by occasional magazine and newspaper articles and the ensuing modest correspondence. Significantly, there was broad political support for the proposal the prospects for which were boosted considerably by a joint Anglo-Irish and EC report, the Erne Catchment Study, which was endorsed by the Economic and Social Committee of the EC in 1983. Towards the end of that year the OPW was given approval to set up a team to carry out a detailed feasibility study and to give a cost estimate. This was carried out over the ensuing two years, a report being prepared in 1986.

A Thorough Survey

It was necessary at the outset of this study to define some parameters of a restored waterway. John McMahon's 1840s design, which formed the basis for most but not all of the original works was for a navigation rising 24m [80ft] from the Shannon, through eight locks, to the summit level and then falling, again through eight locks, 21m [70ft] to the Erne. Design navigation depth at summer flow was 1.8m [6ft], subsequently lowered to 1.4m [4ft6in] for most of the channel and even lower where it turned out not to be possible to reach even 1.4m. Bridge headroom (based on design navigation level) was 4m [13ft].

The OPW engineers' proposals maintained the original headroom and adopted a navigation depth of 1.4m plus 0.3m [approximately 4ft6in plus 1ft], the latter being an allowance for boats 'squatting' while travelling at navigation speed. The channel width would be 13m [42ft6in] wide at the navigation level. The initial investigations showed that on the lengthy eastern section from Castlefore to the Erne, where the main shortcomings of the original venture had occurred, the channel as it had survived was inadequate in both width and depth.

Questions of Water

The question of water levels — how they varied from drought to high flood conditions, how they should be taken into account in the design to accommodate the needs of drainage and navigation, and so on — was a vital one, and the OPW undertook a major hydrological investigation of the whole catchment of the Ballinamore Canal. Among the specific aims of the investigation were the analysis of the effects of alternative possible designs on the lake systems along the waterway, on the ways in which they would meet the needs of navigation, and on the effects on the terminal Erne and Shannon systems. For its report the OPW had available 13 years' hydrometric data from the various flow gauging stations in the catchment.

One of the major influences on the flow regime in the river section [the Lough Scur-Shannon section being a controlled still-water canal without tributaries] would be the consequential effect of the restoration of a navigation depth at the cills of the locks, not only at either end of the summit level but at the remaining seven locks from Ballyduff to the Erne. This required a detailed study, with extensive use of computer modelling.

Central to any design would be the role of the summit level which is the main supply for most canals or canalised rivers. In the case of the Ballinamore Canal this is effectively Lough Scur, the relatively short channels to the lake from Kilclare and Castlefore being minor factors. It has been noted earlier that the diversions of the Kiltubrid [Driny] and Aghacashlaun Rivers were carried out by McMahon to augment the capacity of Lough Scur to handle lockages of boats from the summit level through its terminal locks, while maintaining

The old Accommodation Bridge at Lisnatullagh in 1970. This was not replaced in the reconstruction
Drumany Accommodation Bridge, the only iron lattice bridge, in 1970

the navigation depth for boats traversing the lake itself.

It was maintained at the time of the original construction that the water supply from Lough Scur would be sufficient to cater for the most optimistic estimates of traffic on the waterway, and any possible concerns on this account were assuaged as the 1850s progressed and it became increasingly evident that traffic would be modest at best. Yet the possible inadequacy of the summit level supply has often been quoted as one of the mortal flaws of the original waterway. It is thus interesting to note that the OPW studies showed that there would have been water supply problems for the estimated pleasure boat traffic in the unusually dry years of the mid-1970s.

From the viewpoint of navigation the most critical periods are those of low flow when levels may be such that, as happens at times even on the Shannon, navigation is impeded or restricted. For that to happen, other than in exceptional conditions, on a waterway link such as the Ballinamore Canal would be a major disadvantage. Thus the OPW experts paid a great deal of attention to Lough Scur and the various factors which would influence its adequacy as a water supply. Among the latter were the design criteria for the weir at No 8 Lock, the east-side terminal lock at Castlefore, the degree of evaporation from a relatively wide expanse of virtually still water, the extent of losses of water from leakage and seepage, the outflow through the fishpass at Castlefore, and the consumption of water by lockage of boats.

A computer model was used to assess the likely ability of Lough Scur to accommodate the passing of 25 boats in each direction (with an assumed total of 20 lock openings) per day for the period from 1974 to 1986. The results were revealing:

Lough Scur Summer Performance [1974-1986] [Computed]

Year	Performance	No. of Days of Supply Failure	Year	Performance	No. of Days of Supply Failure
1974	Pass	Nil	1981	Pass	Nil
1975	Fail	99	1982	Marginal*	Nil
1976	Fail	32	1983	Fail	28
1977	Fail	19	1984	Marginal*	Nil
1978	Pass	Nil	1985	Pass	Nil
1979	Marginal*	Nil	1986	Pass	Nil
1980	Pass	Nil			

* Navigation depth not below 1.45m.

As the OPW engineers noted, 'this would mean that the navigation system would have to close during the very summers which would be the most attractive for cruising purposes [the dry summers of 1975/76/77 and 1983] unless some means of flow augmentation was provided.' The latter was then addressed and two possibilities were considered practicable.

The first was to use Carrickaport Lough, located just to the west of Lough Scur, as a reserve supply. By placing a suitable weir at the lake outlet and installing a sluice valve which would be closed in winter, to allow water to accumulate, and would be opened manually and left open when the navigation depth in Lough Scur fell to 1.5 metres, the boat traffic (as assumed for the modelling) would be unimpeded. Without such a valve the use of Carrickaport Lough would have little beneficial effect on the navigation.

The other alternative was to install a pump at Castlefore Lock and backpump water to Lough Scur from the lengthy level to Ballyduff. This includes the St John's Lough system and has a catchment area double that of the summit. Such a system of backpumping is in use on the Lough Allen Canal, as restored from the Shannon at Battle Bridge to the tiny Acres Lough. This system would also ensure uninterrupted navigation on the waterway in very dry weather.

The OPW Design Proposals

The OPW considered the design of the waterway itself under the headings of its three 'natural' sections — the still-water canal from the Shannon to Kilclare, the summit level, and the canalised river section from Castlefore to the Erne. On the first-mentioned section the principal works were the following:

(i) Deepening and rock excavation in the short reach from the Shannon junction to just upstream of Leitrim Bridge.

(ii) As the 8 locks to Kilclare were generally in good condition it was hoped that repairs [repointing and grouting] would make them watertight and serviceable.

(iii) New lock gates with hydraulic sluices would be fitted.

(iv) Nine bridges would be repaired, one rebuilt and one would have its deck raised.

(v) Embankments would be reconstructed and the back drains excavated and relocated in places.

(vi) Overflow weirs would be repaired.

(vii) Mooring facilities would be provided above and below locks and at ends of narrow rock cuts.

The principal design considerations for the Kilclare-Castlefore summit level were the height OD [above Ordnance Datum] of the water level in Lough Scur and the means by which the water supply would be maintained in dry years. A height of 67.0 metres OD — the original navigation level of 220ft — was chosen as the most economic option. As a raised level it would minimise the dredging and rock excavation requirements. On the question of supply augmentation pumping was considered more reliable than the Carrickaport lake storage, but the question was left open for further consideration of economic aspects.

For the river section drainage aspects would be an important consideration.

For example, the actual canalised channel would also serve as the principal drainage artery of the district, while its tributary streams would likewise carry off water from upland areas. It was decided to make the average summer water level such that drainage would be provided for adjacent callows and that the lake levels as they existed would be maintained insofar as it was possible, so that current amenity uses could continue.

The weir crest heights were arranged to permit the tributaries to discharge in summer, while retaining normal winter flood waters within the banks. An amenity consideration was to keep the water levels sufficiently high to permit boat crews to enjoy the views of the countryside through which they were passing. For hydraulic reasons, based on a detailed analysis, it was decided to retain the original weir lengths, with the sluices incorporated in them.

The design envisaged the relocation of three locks and two weirs. The very remote lock at Corraquill [Caroul; No 1] would be moved, with its weir, 600 metres upstream (towards Ballyconnell). This was partly for ease of convenient access and construction, but particularly so that the inflowing Derrylaney River would be below the lock. The lock at Ballyconnell [No 2] would also be moved upstream, nearer the town, from its somewhat remote original location, while the weir would remain at its old site, but with a lowered crest. Finally, the lock and weir at Ballinamore would be moved 750 metres upstream (towards Ballyduff), saving a significant amount of rock excavation. Also, the new design was such that no excavation would be needed upstream of the new lock, in the reach where the original construction had such difficulties with slipping banks and 'rising bottoms.'

As regards the bridges on this section, it was planned that three would have to be rebuilt because of inadequate headroom [those at Cloncoohy, Burren (Coologe) and Lisnatullagh], two would be replaced by lifting bridges [Muckros, south of St John's Lough, and Dernagore, to the east of Cloncoohy], and two old railway bridges [at Derryginny and Aghoo West], also without adequate headroom, would have their single iron spans removed. The remaining bridges would have to be underpinned and repaired.

The locks on the river section had survived the decades in very poor condition. All would be replaced with new chambers 6m [20ft] wide and 26m [85ft] long, of reinforced concrete portal frame construction with double pairs of steel lock gates, and sluices incorporated in the side walls. Weirs would be repaired or, where necessary, replaced by new weirs with sluices and fish passes.

It was estimated that 750,000 cubic metres of material would have to be excavated from the waterway channel, virtually all in the river section. The removal of the material would be carried out under water by dragline which, it was hoped, would eliminate any problems with the rising bottoms which had so bedevilled the original construction. The total included 40,000 cubic metres of rock, the removal of which, mainly just downstream of Garadice

The old Weir at Ballyconnell

The sole surviving Lockhouse, at Ballyconnell, seen in 1970

Lough, would not constitute a problem. The channel through the chain of lakes below Garadice [Ballymagauran (Ballymagovern), Derrycassan and Coologe Loughs] would have to be made by dredging and it was thought that because of the shallowness of all three that continuing dredging would form a key element of the future maintenance of the navigation.

Finally, the design included the rebuilding or modification of the quays at Ballyconnell, Ballinamore and Leitrim, along with the provision of new moorings in Garadice Lough and at Lough Scur, close to Keshcarrigan; there would be 50 mooring spaces in all. Navigation beacons would be provided to mark the navigation channel through the larger lakes.

The OPW engineers were of the opinion that the work on the waterway could be carried out in five stages, each of which was self-contained and had a desirable destination in its own right. These were:

1. Lough Erne to Ballyconnell
2. Ballyconnell to Garadice Lough
3. Garadice Lough to Ballinamore
4. Ballinamore to Lough Scur
5. Lough Scur to the River Shannon.

The cost of each stage, at 1986 prices, was estimated to lie in the range £2-4 million, or a total of £16.5 million, and the timescale for completion (without intervals between stages) at 5 years from commencement. The report was furnished to the Minister for Finance, who told the parliament in May that because of the estimated cost of restoration it was therefore not a viable project.

Proposals Take Shape

That was the position as far as purely national resources were concerned. But in the late 1980s a number of factors coalesced to change the situation rapidly. The International Fund for Ireland was established; North-South cooperation was at a high level; the Structural Fund of the European Community had been established; cross-border projects were being favourably regarded, particularly if there were a Community dimension to them; and, not least, in the South, the prime minister, An Taoiseach, Mr C.J. Haughey, had a deep personal interest in the plans for the revival of the Ballinamore Canal. Much as a jigsaw puzzle is assembled, sections of the picture were being put together in connection with the restoration of the canal in the 1988-90 period, the general position taking shape well before completion of the overall picture.

The spotlight of publicity was again turned on the derelict canal in this period. A team of three journalists from the *Irish Times* made an expedition by canoe to the canal in 1987 and reported daily on their difficult, if not exactly hazardous, journey. They were following in the wake of an earlier team whose voyage, again by canoe, was reported fully, with many colour photographs, in the Aer Lingus in-flight magazine, thereby achieving major exposure.

Early in 1989 the Irish Government decided that matters had developed sufficiently to warrant the preparation of a detailed technical and economic investigation of the restoration being made, and that it would put together a funding portfolio. The decision was taken that the task of executing the project would be given to a subsidiary of the Electricity Supply Board, ESB International, which had much experience of major engineering projects. While this was a considerable disappointment to the OPW, particularly in view of both its historic and recent involvements with the waterway, it had the satisfaction of knowing that its 1986 design scheme formed the cornerstone, as ESBI engineers put it, of the initial project outline for funding purposes. Further, the OPW would, jointly with the Department of Agriculture in Northern Ireland, control and maintain the restored navigation as part of its overall remit as keeper of the national waterway heritage.

By mid-1989 the proposals for funding were taking shape. A report on the financial viability of the navigation, in terms of its contribution to the tourism economy, was commissioned by the International Fund for Ireland which had, in September 1988, been requested by the Irish and British Governments 'to consider the re-opening of the canal as one of its flagship projects'. The IFI report was presented to the Minister for Tourism & Transport by Mr James Doherty, a member of the IFI board. He considered that the study, compiled by Indecon (Ireland) Ltd, was a useful step in bringing the project to fruition and said that the board had earmarked £1 million from its funds to be used for the reopening, subject to the availability of the necessary complementary funding from other sources.

Shortly afterwards the *Irish Times* noted that 'the Government has high-profiled the scheme in its package of proposals to win money from the new structural funds' of the EC. By this time commitments to the funding had been made by the IFI, both Governments and the Electricity Supply Board.

Because of the necessity to have an accurate costing for the funding proposal, ESBI were engaged from the earliest possible date on the preparation of a detailed design scheme on which a more exact estimate of costs would be based. While the OPW had estimated the cost in 1986 at some £16 million, its scheme (while differing in technical detail aspects from the ESBI proposals, as

---

CANAL CONSTRUCTION

LTD

(A Subsidiary of Electricity Supply Board)

BALLINAMORE AND

BALLYCONNELL CANAL

LOUGH SCUR CONTRACT

Tenders are invited for the initial contract on the restoration of the canal. The main works of this contract comprise earthworks over a one kilometre length of the canal and refurbishment of a weir.

Tender documents are available for the Purchasing Manager, Electricity Supply Board, 27 Lr Fitzwilliam Street, Dublin 2 subject to the provision of a deposit of IR£1,000, this deposit to be refundable on receipt of a bona fide tender not subsequently withdrawn. Cheques should be made payable to Canal Construction Ltd.

It will be a condition of the Contract that the successful contractor and any subcontractor(s) each produce a valid C2 Certificate, a Tax C' :rance Certificate or a statement from the Irish Revenue Commissioners as to their suitability for appointment.

The lowest or any Tender will not necessarily be accepted.

The latest date for the receipt of sealed Tenders will be 3 p.m. on September 21st, 1990.

Notice of the initial
Reconstruction Contract

noted below) had not been as comprehensive in its overall coverage as ESBI now proposed, and had been to some extent preliminary.

One factor which ESBI had to take particular account of was the making of the European Communities (Environmental Impact Assessment) Regulations, 1989 — and similar regulations in Northern Ireland — which governed the making of an environmental impact assessment and the issuing of an Environmental Impact Statement [EIS]. This reconstruction was the first public project undertaken in accordance with the Regulations.

Thus, in the latter half of 1989, preparations were in hand on a number of fronts. The detailed environmental impact assessment was under way; up-to-date costings were being prepared; the mammoth task of preparing a detailed design (based on exhaustive surveys and investigations) was being undertaken; land acquisition procedures were being drawn up. The Government was preparing the funding portfolio, and its legal officers were drafting the legislation under which the project would be carried out. [In Northern Ireland the existing drainage legislation covered the project.] By the end of the year it was reckoned that reconstruction would require three years and the expenditure of £30 million, based on an un-phased approach in which the whole canal would be tackled as a single project.

Cruising the reconstructed waterway in April 1994.
Photo: Frank Miller, The Irish Times.

THE OFFICE OF PUBLIC WORKS

NOTICE NO. 1D

SHANNON NAVIGATION ACT, 1990

COMPULSORY ACQUISITION OF LAND

1. The Commissioners of Public Works in Ireland (referred to subsequently in this Notice as "the Commissioners") hereby give notice that, in exercise of the powers conferred on them, by sections 2 and 5 of and the Schedule to the Shannon Navigation Act, 1990 (No. 20 of 1990), they propose to acquire compulsorily, for the purposes of their functions in relation to the Shannon Navigation, the land described in the Schedule to this notice.

2. Maps showing the land intended to be acquired by the Commissioners as aforesaid, together with a list showing the reputed owners and occupiers of the land, are deposited in the Garda Siochana Stations at Belturbet and at Ballyconnell in the County of Cavan and may be inspected at any of those stations by members of the public at all reasonable times.

3. An occupier or owner or mortgagee of any of the land may submit an objection to its acquisition as aforesaid to the Commissioners at 51 St. Stephen's Green, Dublin 2 on or before the 8th day of April, 1991.

FIRST SCHEDULE

Description of the land proposed to be acquired

The lands of the Ballinamore and Ballyconnell Navigation and riparian lands between Lough Erne and Ballyconnell as more particularly detailed on the maps and schedules deposited and shown as Lots Nos. D0 to D48 in the Townlands of Coragh, Corgreagh, Corraback, Corraghquill, Cuillaghan, Drumgart, Kilcorky, Lagan and Mullanwary in the Barony of Lower Loughtee and County of Cavan and in the Townlands of Annagh, Cullyleenan, Derryginny, Doon, Gortawee or Scotchtown and Rakeelan in the Barony of Tullyhaw and County of Cavan.

Dated this 7th day of February, 1991.

THE OFFICE OF PUBLIC WORKS

NOTICE NO. A1

SHANNON NAVIGATION ACT, 1990
COMPULSORY ACQUISITION OF LAND

The Commissioners of Public Works in Ireland (referred to subsequently in this Notice as "the Commissioners") hereby give notice that, in exercise of the powers conferred on them by sections 2 and 5 of and the Schedule to the Shannon Navigation Act, 1990 (No. 20 of 1990), they propose to acquire compulsorily, for the purposes of their functions in relation to the Shannon navigation, the land described in the Schedule to this notice.

Maps showing the land intended to be acquired by the Commissioners as aforesaid together with a list showing the reputed owners and occupiers of the land is deposited in the Garda Siochana Stations at Ballinamore and Keshcarrigan in the county of Leitrim and at Ballyconnell in the county of Cavan and may be inspected at any of those stations by members of the public at all reasonable times.

An occupier or owner of any of the land aforesaid may submit an objection to its acquisition as aforesaid to the Commissioners at 51 St Stephen's Green, Dublin 2 or on or before the 28th day of February, 1991.

SCHEDULE

Description of the land proposed to be acquired

The lands of the Ballinamore Ballyconnell Navigation and riparian lands between the River Shannon and the Eighth Lock in the townlands of Kilmacsherwell and Kiltyfinnan as more particularly detailed on the maps and schedules deposited and shown as Lots No. A0 to A115 in the Townlands of Ballinwing, Corglass, Driny, Drumaleague, Drumcong, Drumduff South, Drumruekill, Gowly, Keshcarrigan, Kilclare Beg, Kilclare More, Killarcan, Leitrim, Letterfine, Loughconway, Loughscur, Newbrook, Roscarban, Rossy, Scrabbagh, Seltan (Moran), Seltan (McDonald), Sheffield, Tirmactiernan and Tullylanan, in the Barony of Leitrim and County of Leitrim and Boneill, Gubroe, Kilmacsherwell and Kiltyfinnan in the Barony of Mohill and County of Leitrim.

Dated this 19th day of December, 1990.

THE OFFICE OF PUBLIC WORKS

Right: The first Compulsory Land Acquisition Notice, 19 Dec 1990. Left: Land Acquisition notice of 7 Feb 1991 for Navigation and Riparian Lands between Lough Erne and Ballyconnell

CANAL CONSTRUCTION LTD.

(A Subsidiary of Electricity Supply Board)

BALLINAMORE AND BALLYCONNELL CANAL STILLWATER CONTRACT

Tenders are invited for the Stillwater Contract on the restoration of the canal. The main works comprise construction of low embankments, deepening and widening of channel, bridge repairs, lock repairs, installation of moorings and pumped water supply system.

Tender documents are available from the Purchasing Manager, Electricity Supply Board, 27 Lr. Fitzwilliam Street, Dublin 2, subject to the provision of a deposit of IR£1,000, this deposit to be refundable on receipt of a bona fide tender not subsequently withdrawn. Cheques should be made payable to Canal Construction Ltd.

It will be a condition of the Contract that the successful contractor and any subcontractor(s) each produce a valid C2 Certificate, a Tax Clearance Certificate or a statement from the Irish Revenue Commissioners as to their suitability for appointment.

The lowest or any Tender will not necessarily be accepted.

The latest date for the receipt of sealed Tenders will be 3 pm on 4th January 1991.

CANAL CONSTRUCTION LTD.
(a Subsidiary of Electricity Supply Board)

BALLINAMORE AND BALLYCONNELL CANAL

ERNE TO GARADICE EARTH WORKS CONTRACT

Tenders are invited for the Erne to Garadice Earthworks Contract on the restoration of the canal. The main works comprise deepening and widening of existing river channel, lake dredging, weir construction, installation of moorings, underpinning and bridge remedial works.

Tender documents are available from the Purchasing Manager, Electricity Supply Board, 27 Lr. Fitzwilliam Street, Dublin 2, subject to the provision of a deposit of £1,000, this deposit to be refundable on receipt of a bonafide tender not subsequently withdrawn. Cheques should be made payable to Canal Construction Ltd.

It will be a condition of the Contract that the successful contractor and any subcontractor(s) each produce a valid C2 Certificate, a Tax Clearance Certificate or a statement from the Irish Revenue Commissioners as to their suitability for appointment.

The lowest or any Tender will not necessarily be accepted.

The latest date for the receipt of sealed Tenders will be 3 pm on 15th March 1991.

Above: Notice of a major Earthworks Contract

Left: Contract Notice for the Restoration of the Still-Water Canal

Below: The former Aghalane Bridge, looking from north to south in 1970

CHAPTER 5

THE PROJECT IS REALISED

The latter half of 1989 was a period of major activity for ESBI, in particular, as ideas, proposals and plans had to be finalized so that the Government could prepare definitive funding proposals, based on a comprehensive design for the restoration. Given the availability of the necessary finance it was the firm intention to complete the entire project within a three-year construction period, starting early in 1991. Approval at EC level would be contingent on a satisfactory Environmental Impact Statement [EIS], and the necessary assessment of the project in all its environmental aspects was one of the first tasks put in hand. As sponsors of this major cross-border initiative, the Irish and British Governments were jointly the clients for whom all works would be carried out. They were represented by a Joint Steering Committee of officials from the appropriate departments of either government.

The preparation of the environmental impact assessment was a most pressing early matter because of the many stages involved, including the necessarily somewhat protracted consultative process, before final approval of the resulting EIS. A scoping report, in which the projected coverage of the assessment was set out, was completed by mid-1989, leaving the rest of the year for the necessary surveys and inquiries and the drafting of the EIS. The primary topics highlighted in the scoping report for study were the socio-economic aspects of the project, drainage considerations, water quantity and quality aspects, the ecology of the catchment, and the impact on landscape. A wide range of organizations was consulted during the environmental assessment; many were state agencies but the opinions of voluntary bodies north and south were also canvassed.

In a depressed area such as the catchment of the waterway the probable social and economic influences of the reconstruction would be a big consideration, and these were specifically addressed by a baseline survey. Counties Cavan and Leitrim, especially the latter, have suffered greatly over a long period from depopulation and it was important to ascertain if the decline could be arrested or even reversed by the benefits accruing from the canal.

The study found that three-quarters of the increased revenue from tourism, as a consequence of the project, would benefit the immediate catchment area and that it would indeed help to revitalize the area.

The so-called beneficial uses of a river system, much more than a pure canal, can be many and varied. They include drainage and flood relief, fisheries, water supply for domestic and/or industrial use, boating, general amenity uses (such as walking along the banks, bird watching and so on), controlled disposal of effluents and the like. All were considered in the assessment and a compromise between the sometimes conflicting uses devised. The approach adopted was one whereby all the relevant beneficial uses were catered for within a satisfactory range of conditions.

The greatest difficulty in reconciling conflicting beneficial uses arises in the cases of maintaining water quality (and consequently a habitat suitable for fish, especially game fish) and of the disposal of waste. Studies of water quality along the river channel showed generally satisfactory conditions, though not pristine, and to prevent deterioration caused by sewage discharges from boats it was decided that all principal mooring areas should be provided with sewage pumpout facilities for cruisers and with waste disposal facilities. Boats are prohibited under by-law from discharging sewage into the waterway.

A Sensitive Environment

The environmental studies showed that there were five areas of special botanical interest along the route, all of which demanded protection. One endangered species — the marsh pea — was found near Upper Lough Erne. Notably, the waterway is of international importance for wintering wildfowl — a significant proportion of the world population of whooper swans, which breed in Iceland, winter along it, as do other species. Also, although a population of brown trout inhabits the navigation (mainly at Ballyconnell), the river system as a whole is a good coarse fishery.

Suitable protection of flora and fauna was achieved by ensuring that dredging and/or excavation was carried out at sensitive locations from within the channel and not from either bank. Depending on the conditions applying at each of these sites material was removed either by machinery on floating pontoons or by machines in the water course which were given raised cabs. Material removed was brought by barge to one of a dozen or so designated spoil disposal locations — lands which were acquired temporarily for the purpose, the procedure being that the topsoil was removed, the spoil from the waterway deposited and spread, the topsoil restored and the lands returned to their owners. This was a very practical and successful course of action.

It was decided that outside these special areas, for a combination of engineering and environmental reasons, excavation would be from one bank only wherever possible, the other bank remaining unworked. Also, the unstable nature of the soils in many areas, where slippage of worked banks with normal slopes was a potential problem, dictated that gentle slopes should be made on the worked side. Thus, at many reaches along the waterway there is one relatively steep bank and one which slopes more gently.

Progress on all Fronts

Concurrently with the environmental study a series of site investigations and site trials was devised and commenced. These yielded much data which benefited the final design. These various inquiries were duly reported on to the Joint Steering Committee, which at the beginning of 1990 received the all-important cost plan and the EIS, both of which were issued in January 1990. The EC engaged independent UK consultants to audit the cost, environmental and technical findings, all of which were endorsed without alteration and adopted for implementation. The final approved budget was £30 million.

A legal basis for the reconstruction was given by the Shannon Navigation Act, 1990, passed in June. Under its provisions the Ballinamore and Ballyconnell Canal and the so-called Erne & Lough Oughter Navigation [i.e. the Erne River southwards to Belturbet] became part of the Shannon Navigation and subject to its legislation. The Ballinamore and Ballyconnell Navigation Trustees, established by Act of 1856, were abolished — by this time a purely nominal event — and their powers and functions were transferred to the OPW, which received additional powers in relation to land acquisition and the making of by-laws. The function of reconstructing the waterway was delegated to the ESB in August 1990 for three years. The delegation was renewed for a further two years in August 1993.

The planning and management of the reconstruction required a high degree of co-ordination of the many separate, but ultimately complementary activities, so that each was in phase with the others to eliminate hold-ups. This was a major responsibility of ESBI which was appointed Project Manager. It was also the principal consultant for the work, undertaking the enormous task of designing the reconstruction. It was aided by Kirk McClure & Morton, of Belfast, as sub-consultants. The designated constructors of the waterway were Canal Construction Company Ltd of Dublin, a subsidiary of the ESB.

The project was divided into a series of contracts, so that keen competitive international tendering was achieved, as required by EC law. The first contract, let in late 1990, was the 'Lough Scur Contract', for earthworks over a one kilometre length of the canal and refurbishing of a weir [at Castlefore]. This was something of a pilot exercise to clarify construction methods and the requirements of landowners. The 'Stillwater Contract', involving the construction of low embankments, deepening and widening of channel, bridge repairs, lock repairs, installation of moorings and pumped water supply system, was let in spring 1991. The remaining, major contracts were for either earthworks

or structures, and were valued around £2.5 million each. The principal contractors were: Pat Mulcair Civil Engineering; Pierse Contracting; Jones Civil
Engineering; M.J. Lambe & Sons; CW Land & Marine; Process Control and
Automation Systems; and SIAC. Together they were responsible for executing
the following works:

EARTHWORKS AND EXCAVATION: Deepening and widening sections of the
Woodford River channel and the still-water canal; protecting banks with rock-armour
where necessary and with timber piles in soft ground; lining the bed and banks at
Kilclare to prevent leakage of water; carrying out the work from one bank only, where
possible, and using floating plant to stay clear of the land altogether in environmentally
sensitive areas so that natural habitats were preserved; major dredging of Ballymagauran [Ballymagovern] Lake and Upper Lough Erne plus minor dredging of the
access to five other lakes, with transportation of spoil to designated land-based areas.
BRIDGES: Replacing (or, less frequently, altering) minor concrete bridges; underpinning and making major repairs to masonry structures.
LOCKS: Reconstructing eight lock chambers in reinforced concrete and cladding with
original masonry; repairing the remaining eight locks; providing all sixteen locks with
new automated gates and sluices; installing pumps at each of the eight locks leading
from the Shannon, and at Castlefore lock on the Woodford River, to pump water up
to summit level. [All locks are either on or very close to their original sites; there was
no relocation of locks as had been envisaged in the OPW design].
WEIRS: Rebuilding weirs and fish passes at all locks on the Woodford River section;
constructing weirs and by-pass channels at four locks between the Shannon and Lough
Scur.
MOORINGS: Constructing concrete moorings above and below each lock for crew
access; providing six public mooring areas with berthing facilities, sewage pump-out
facilities, water supply, service block with shower, toilets and laundry room; refuse
disposal.
MISCELLANEOUS: Electrofishing and removal of fish to safe havens during the works
and restocking on completion; landscaping and planting along the worked river banks
and mooring areas; provision of services to adjoining farm lands now separated from
waterway, such as water supply for animals; drainage; access etc.

The major quantities were: soft excavation 800,000 cu m; rock excavation
150,000 cu m; concrete 25,000 cu m; structural steelwork 220 tonnes; 11,000
timber piles and 11,150 cu m of rock armour (for bank support); and access
roads 5.5km approximately.

Lands are Acquired

Procedures for land acquisition were developed in 1989 and preliminary
consultations were held with landowners and their representatives. The OPW
was responsible for the permanent acquisition, in accordance with the 1990
Act, where necessary by compulsory purchase, of the lands required for the
waterway, including the channel, the lakes, the original canal banks and any

Widening in progress on the Letterfine Rock Cut, looking towards Lough Scur. Note that work is confined to one bank [ESBI]
Work in progress at Killarcan Lock [No 16], showing the fine inverted arch [ESBI]

additional lands needed. ESBI prepared the surveys for over 400 acquisitions. Separate ESB notices for the early entry onto lands were prepared in each case in accordance with the Act. These were issued to landowners, lease holders and mortgagees and they were also posted on the land. They provided information on the extent of work proposed on the land with an accompanying map. A small proportion of the acquisitions were contested in the District Courts with one appeal to the Circuit Court.

Each landowner was visited and conditions of entry agreed. Fencing and water supply were issues which required extensive consultation and where possible a piped water supply to cattle troughs was provided at sections where lands were fenced from the canal. In all, consultations were held with over 500 landowners and occupiers. This was a daunting but ultimately rewarding task, as the land transfers proceeded without any of the major problems which had been envisaged as far back as a century ago. Its success reflected credit on all concerned. The total area of property involved was about 465 hectares, the cost of its acquisition being some £800,000.

The Water Supply

The most important consideration in the design of a navigation is the adequacy of the proposed water supply. This question had been addressed in depth by the OPW and of course it was dominant in the ESBI planning. A peculiarity of a canalised river navigation is that conditions can, and indeed are likely to, arise where there is at one time too much water and at another time too little. Generally, the latter prevails during the summer navigation season.

The earlier OPW studies had shown that in dry summers the water supply from Lough Scur would fail unless augmentation measures were undertaken; backpumping from the Castlefore-Ballyduff reach was proposed. When it was considering the position ESBI had available an additional three years' flow records. These showed that the 1989 outflow from Lough Scur had been as low as in the very dry 1975 and that a considerable degree of pumping would have been needed to maintain navigability. In fact, there was a danger that continuing pumping from the river section beyond Castlefore would have caused a reversal of the flow regime in the stretch. The decision was therefore taken to install two 80 litre/second pumps below each of the locks on the still-water section to permit additional water to be pumped to the summit level from the Shannon which has a relatively large catchment at Leitrim Village.

Having determined that the water supply would be sufficient to handle all demands in dry seasons, excluding leakage of water which was addressed during construction, the next requirement was to ensure that the waterway would have sufficient depth for the boats using it. An extensive survey of existing boats, and those projected for use, on the Erne and Shannon Navigations, showed that over 90% had a draught of 1.2m or less. Accordingly, a minimum depth of water of 1.55mm was chosen, allowing 1.2m for the boat draught and 0.35m for squat and weed growth. Although it is the case that in many sections of the waterway the depth is likely to exceed the contract minimum of 1.55m, the maximum draught for boats on the system is fixed by by-law at 1.25m.

The other limiting dimensions of the navigation channel are: width at summer navigation level [the summer mean water level during non-flood periods] 13m, width at bottom 8m. The speed limit is 5km/hour. At bridges the minimum headroom over summer navigation level is 3.65m over a 3.0m width. The limiting factor for headroom is the height of the original masonry bridges, which were repaired and renovated but not altered structurally. Headroom is often greater at the minor bridges which were replaced or raised.

The navigation rules quote the 'navigation criteria' as the following recommended maxima: draught 1.2m; width 4.5m; length 24m; height above water line 3.2m over a 3m width. In regard to the last figure a warning is given that boats 3.2m or higher may not have sufficient headroom under bridges. Should an extremely wet summer occur, with a consequent rise in water levels either on the Shannon, which flows back under Leitrim Bridge to Lock 16, or along the waterway, then it could happen exceptionally that navigation could be restricted or suspended for boats demanding maximum headroom, during the duration of the floods.

Although the Shannon Navigation is open for navigation all year round, albeit with much restricted access to locks in the off-season, the Shannon-Erne Waterway will effectively be a seasonal navigation. While navigation would in theory be possible in winter, the probability of floods occurring is such as to rule it out on practical grounds. If the flow in the river section is greater than 3.5 knots it will not be possible to travel upstream with a Shannon or Erne cruiser. However, it is difficult to conjure up a picture of even a keen waterway fan attempting a Shannon-Erne cruise in the average Irish winter!

The Navigation Levels

Having determined the dimensional requirements for the navigational channel ESBI had then to decide how to bring them about. Above all it was essential that the summer navigational level would be guaranteed along the length of the system. A key decision was the fixing of this level at 67m OD — as in the original design — on the summit level. This meant that a considerable rise above the actual water levels in Lough Scur in past summers would occur, with its consequent implications for land purchase.

The alternative course of a reduced level in combination with a deepened channel was not favoured because of the necessity for rock excavation at Lough Scur which might cause water leakage through the limestone. Also, the benefits of raising the level at Lough Scur — the storage capacity of the summit level would be increased considerably, and a scenic lake with an interesting history would become available for boats to explore — would be significant.

Water levels on the still-water canal section were fixed as in the original design, except for one reach. Site tests involving the construction of a short raised trial embankment in the short level between Tirmactiernan Lock [No 15] and Killarcan Lock [No 16] had shown conclusively that there would be great difficulty in making higher embankments in order to provide the necessary navigation level. The lesser evil was to lower the channel by deepening, even though this required a greater quantity of rock excavation than originally anticipated and also the underpinning of two locks and a bridge.

East of the summit level differing approaches were adopted according to the circumstances prevailing. In the first reach, from Castlefore through the St John's Lough system to Ballyduff, the level was raised by 0.7m, for a number of environmental and technical reasons, in order to provide a navigation depth. In general, however, it was not considered practicable to restore the old navigation level, mainly because to do so would interfere with the reasonably satisfactory drainage regime which had evolved over the years; it would also have flooded farmland which had been improved consequent on the dropping of the original level. The approach taken was thus to fix the summer navigation level at or near the mean level in recent years and to provide a navigation depth by widening and deepening the old channel. In general, the reconstruction was designed so that existing drainage would not be lessened and any future drainage scheme not interfered with.

The channel from Corraquill Lock [No 1] to Upper Lough Erne is influenced directly by the water levels in the Erne system, and as a consequence the available navigation depth can greatly exceed that elsewhere on the waterway. This is reflected in a feature at Corraquill — the rather lofty new accommodation bridge over the Erne end of the lock. It has a very generous headroom above design navigation level — 5.5m — to provide clearance for boats during those periods when there is a considerable back-up of water from Upper Lough Erne. Another consequence of the variability of water levels in this reach is that the new floating mooring at Aghalane was designed to cope with a 2m range in levels.

Looking for Leaks

A long-standing problem which ESBI had to tackle was that of water loss from the navigation through fissures in the rock formation. Specific tests were carried out at the Letterfine rock cutting, immediately west of Lough Scur, and on the original lock masonry to confirm that they were watertight. No leakage was found at these points. With the water supply on the summit level already somewhat at risk in dry summers, unless augmented, it would be intolerable that any leakage would persist. The waterway is designed so that, except in flood conditions, all water will discharge eastwards to the Erne, and not to either side of the summit, as used happen prior to reconstruction. Discharge westwards though leakage or otherwise has to be avoided.

It has been recounted earlier how Pat Doherty, the Kilclare miller, was able in the 1860s to run his mill all year using the water leaking from the waterway nearby. Clearly, investigation was needed of the rock cut at the Kilclare locks [Nos 9/10/11]. Using an excavator, the rock surface was exposed in this section, revealing actual or potential leak holes for which the chosen remedy was lining of the canal bed. This was achieved by placing plastic sheeting on the bed and banks and protecting it with concrete.

Renewing the Locks

Undoubtedly the most fascinating feature of a waterway, both to user and onlooker, are the locks. Those built for the Ballinamore and Ballyconnell Canal — 16 in all, equally divided between still-water and river sections — were magnificent examples of masonry work, with generous dimensions and generally with considerable rise in level. As the OPW had earlier found, the eight locks nearer the Shannon, on the still-water canal, had survived the decades in relatively good order and, with suitable repairs (sometimes extensive), they would serve the reconstructed navigation.

Renovation included the repointing of all the original masonry and grouting behind it, with occasional replacement of masonry blocks. New concrete cills and quoins were provided, as well as reinforced concrete housing for the hydraulic operating machinery. In addition, concrete floors were required at most while all locks had to be underpinned. Two locks [Nos 15-16, next the Shannon] had to be substantially modified to permit a reduction in navigation water level, in the reach between them, over the original design figure.

All original lock gates had long since disappeared so that two replacement pairs per lock were needed along the whole navigation. Lock operation is now automatic, by means of an electro-hydraulic system described in the next chapter, although the various stages of lock use are under the control of a boat crew member. Thus, all lock gates lack one feature familiar on less up-to-date canals — the lengthy, white-ended balance beams. Weirs and by-pass channels, for the discharge of excess water in floods, were constructed at the first four locks from the Shannon [Nos 13-16], and were provided with walkways or bridges where needed.

Greater effort was required to reinstate the other eight locks, between Lough Scur and the Erne. As constructed, these equally fine locks were each complemented by a weir with a large sluice for the discharge of flood waters, the latter being located at the end of the weir nearer the lock. When, in time, lock gates and sluices disappeared, water levels dropped and the weirs — designed to ease the discharge of excess water — now acted as retaining walls which served to divert the entire river flow through the lock chamber and the gap between weir and masonry-walled island next the lock which had formerly housed the sluice. Thus the masonry works were under a dual assault from unchecked flood waters for over a century and they suffered greatly.

Much of the masonry work was considerably loosened if not seriously damaged — the lock at Ballinamore was in a particularly precarious position — and the channel bed at several locations was littered with masonry blocks displaced from both locks and weirs. Reconstruction rather than repair was necessary, although the new, larger than original, reinforced concrete locks were carefully clad above summer navigation level with the original masonry, To facilitate this retention of the original appearance of the locks, the earlier structures were carefully dismantled each block being numbered for reuse; all displaced masonry was retrieved from the channel.

Weirs and Bridges

Some of the original stone weirs had survived quite intact but others had been broken, possibly deliberately in order to reduce flood levels. However, because of the redesign of the works on the river section (in which no sluices would be provided, except at one location), it was decided to build new concrete weirs at each of the eight locations. These are not masonry clad as all the concrete work, save for the new fish passes, is under water and not in view.

As will be noted in the next chapter, the bridges prior to reconstruction varied from the sublime to the unspeakable. The former were the masonry bridges, mostly with a single arch, straight or skewed [but with two interesting exceptions]; the latter were ramshackle accommodation bridges, a couple of which at least were post-Award and unofficial. It was decided that in order to preserve the ambience of a Victorian navigation none of the masonry bridges would be replaced and that whatever repairs or modifications were needed in accordance with the new design would be carried out.

The remaining bridges, a couple of post-Award additions apart, were originally wooden or iron structures, mostly on masonry abutments, which had not survived the years well. Indeed, all had been replaced, some on more than one occasion, usually with flat concrete spans which were very basic but served their purpose adequately. As there was no necessity for it, virtually all the replacement structures offered inadequate or negligible headroom for boats. Most of these bridges were replaced by new concrete structures, others having their decks raised. Where practicable the altered or replacement bridges were clad with old masonry in order to harmonize with the original masonry arch bridges.

Immediately prior to reconstruction there were 34 bridges along the waterway. Five of these — two old railway bridges and three accommodation bridges — were removed as redundant through disuse or by negotiation, and were not replaced, while two additional accommodation bridges were provided at locks for boat users and walkers. The current total number of bridges is, accordingly, 31, one of which has been preserved in a ruined state.

To improve accessibility and to encourage non-boating amenity uses of the waterway, such as angling, walking along the banks, study of flora and fauna, an unmetalled tow-path has been provided along virtually the whole of the navigation, lake shores excepted. However, walkers at most of the principal bridges no longer have tow-paths underneath, a very minor inconvenience, as these were largely removed in order to widen the navigation channel through them.

Kilclare Middle Lock [No 10; Drumruekill], showing detail of the new gates [ESBI]
Below: Constructing the new Lock [No 8] and Bridge at Castlefore [ESBI]

Attractive Amenities

Boat users, too, now have available a range of welcome amenities. As originally built the waterway had wharves at only three locations — Leitrim, Ballinamore and Ballyconnell, the three principal settlements along its course. Requests or suggestions for further moorings or quays made in the 1850s were refused. While these might have sufficed for a trade navigation, they would not cater at all adequately for the leisurely traffic on a pleasure cruising waterway. The reconstruction thus included the provision of comprehensive, modern facilities at the three original sites and at three new strategic locations — Aghalane, near the Erne, Haughton's Shore at Garadice Lake [Ballinacur], and Keshcarrigan, at the eastern entry to Lough Scur.

While there are short concrete moorings above and below each lock, these are primarily to facilitate landing and boarding in connection with lock operations. The six new public moorings are much more extensive, especially at Ballinamore, and boast a range of amenities and utilities. Not least of the attractions at these moorings is their pleasant, tranquil setting which will add greatly to the delights of navigating the waterway.

The restoration project has also added greatly to the attractions of the towns it serves. The local residents have gained a considerable amenity which will enhance the quality of life, quite apart from any economic benefits. At Ballyconnell, the layout of the navigation features — wharf, bridge, weir and lock — has facilitated the making of an extremely pleasant circular walking route. Ballinamore, too, has an interesting complex of waterway features which will undoubtedly form the venue for many a Sunday walk.

Works are Completed

Work on the re-creation of the navigation was favoured by quite reasonable weather, better than had been hoped for, which meant that the originally planned three-year construction period was cut by about a third. By mid-1993 the waterway was essentially complete, only some fine details remaining to be finished. The earthmoving machinery of the contractors had gone, locks and weirs were complete and in working order, the public moorings and their facilities were virtually finished, bridgeworks and rock excavation had been completed. Test runs along the navigation had been made and cruisers had been brought onto it for evaluation of performance of the new works and, most importantly, for the taking of publicity photographs along the various scenic stretches of its course.

Wisely, it was decided to maintain the planned opening date of spring 1994, and not to attempt a rushed opening in 1993. As has been recounted, the navigation is far from being a simple canal and it was considered important both to let it 'settle down' after the enormous disruption, particularly to the difficult soils, of the construction period, and to ascertain how well the design coped with the discharge of flood waters in the very wet winter of 1993/4. As this book is being completed, the reports are excellent and all has gone very well indeed with traffic having commenced on 2 April 1994 and the formal opening of the Shannon-Erne Waterway on 23 May.

The reconstructed waterway is a striking testimonial to the skills and dedication of all those connected in its planning, design and execution. It is of a standard equal to any in Europe and is a major new asset for this island. It is most pleasing to record, too, that it is also a tribute to those who undertook the corresponding tasks 150 years ago on the original Ballinamore and Ballyconnell Navigation. Today's professionals from ESBI and the OPW are united in their praise of the talents of those who conceived and implemented the original scheme, especially those of John McMahon and William T. Mulvany.

Vindicating the Pioneers

Together the two pioneers created a navigation which was ultimately defeated by forces outside their control, and a drainage system which stood the test of time. They left a fine legacy of masonry structures, many of which they unerringly founded on the sole rock formations to exist at one location after another. They carried out river diversion works which were, and are again, of great benefit in providing a water supply and in minimizing siltation in the navigation. They unknowingly provided an excellent basis for the 1990s reconstruction. Justice demands that these discoveries (for that is what they are) made during the investigations and assessments by both the OPW and ESBI should lead to a reassessment of the status of the original navigation. It has now become clear that the early scheme, instead of being inherently flawed through faulty design and none too careful construction, as has been thought for over a century, was in fact scientifically wellfounded and properly designed. Instead of collapsing internally, as it were, it was defeated by an unassailable combination of external factors.

Undoubtedly the underlying cause of failure was the completion of the main trunk railway lines around the time of the original construction. As the navigation slowly took shape the railway link from Limerick to Dublin to Belfast was already a reality; whatever through traffic there was had already been transferred to rail. As far as local traffic was concerned, it emerged that there was insufficient volume to tempt traders on to the waterway. Claims that local railway competition was a factor are nonsense; the Cavan & Leitrim Railway — which would have been a real threat to a locally successful navigation — was not opened until 1887-88.

As the trunk railways spread, the OPW was facing the ultimately fatal problem, in the then circumstances, of the treacherous soils through which the navigation was being constructed. Excavation was by the primitive techniques of the period — a combination of manpower, shovels and wheelbarrows. This meant that in practical terms spoil removed from the channel had to be deposited along the parallel banks. These were inherently unstable and tended to sink or slip under the weight of deposit, with a loss of bank material back to the channel which rose from its excavated level. This was the accursed phenomenon called 'rising bottoms', which dogged the construction for years.

Excavation was extremely costly; the budgets had long since been overrun; the financial consequences of spoil transport and deposition at points without influence on the banks would not have borne thinking about; the commercial future of the waterway as part of a trunk navigation was clearly in doubt. With hindsight it is small wonder, then, that the OPW faced the facts and decided to stop the works when they did, ending a draining of funds which could have lasted for years.

It is surely a matter of regret that the vindication of those who toiled so valiantly over the navigation of the 1840s and 50s has been such a long time in coming. But, sadly, from the outset there was a stand-off between the OPW and the navigation trustees. The trustees blamed the OPW for every last imperfection in the waterway handed over to them (although some of J.B. Pratt's criticisms must have had substance); the OPW, having rid itself of a major problem, constantly took refuge in the provisions of the Drainage Acts — they were no longer liable. This may have been a technically sound position but it was one which infuriated the trustees and ultimately led to the colour-fully extravagant evidence given by J.G.V. Porter in his day and which resulted in the creation of a myth which persisted for far too long.

It is a pleasure to set the record straight.

Former Tralee & Dingle Light Railway engine No 4T heads a goods train from Arigna and Drumshanbo alongside the navigation between Ballyduff and Ballinamore in 1953 [L. Hyland, courtesy Irish Railway Record Society]

CHAPTER 6

ECOLOGY AND ENVIRONMENT

It has been related elsewhere in this book that the carrying out of the Environmental Impact Assessment in connection with the proposed restoration was a major priority task commenced in mid-1989. As the essential precursor to the making of the Environmental Impact Statement [EIS], the assessment had necessarily to cover every foreseen impact on the environment of the largely unspoilt country in which the waterway is located.

Of the major topics dealt with in detail — and which merit closer examination here — two were the ecology and general environment of the waterway. A comprehensive study of the setting of the navigation was undertaken, in which flora and fauna were each examined in detail and noted so that the appropriate protective measures could be put in place both during and after the construction period. Allied to these studies were the investigations of the water quality and of the possible impacts of the restoration on the landscape.

Water Quality This was found to be satisfactory, as assessed by a suitable range of chemical parameters, with confirmation by biological investigation. A key decision, taken in order to prevent deterioration of water quality, particularly in the primary mooring areas, was that the discharge of sewage from cruisers should be prohibited, and that the services strategically located along the waterway should include pumpout facilities for sewage from craft using the canal. This prohibition on such discharges was subsequently reinforced in the by-laws governing the waterway.

Vegetation It was found that a feature of the waterway was its wetland habitats which were primarily associated with the various lakes scattered along the system. There was a considerable diversity of vegetation communities and a total of five areas of particular interest were identified. Shown on the 'Navigational Charts' for the waterway, these are considered to be especially sensitive areas.

The first is on the Still-Water Canal, near Leitrim Village. It is an irregularly shaped area straddling the navigation channel and is located between 400 and 900 metres from the Shannon — just a little past the new mooring near Leitrim

Bridge. This is the old Black Lough area and it has a very rich channel flora.

Second is an area, to the north of the channel, commencing some 400 metres to the east of Carrickmakeegan Bridge [Bridge No 23] and surrounding the extreme north-west portion of Garadice Lough. It extends to a point some 31.5 km from the Shannon and is also an area of marginal vegetation rich in species. Its existence is attributed to a combination of factors — winter flooding, silt deposition and lack of disturbance by grazing livestock.

The third such area is quite extensive, extending from the southern side of Woodford Lough (just to the east of Ballinacur Bridge), around the tip of Woodford Demesne — including the area of the outfall of the Ballymagauran River — and encompassing a significant area at the south/ south-west shore of Ballymagauran Lough. The total lineal extent is nearly 2 kilometres and it extends to the lake outfall. This area contains the greatest diversity of botanical species found at any one site along the whole waterway.

The fourth area is located below Ballyconnell and is the most extensive and complex. In the stretch from the start of the Scotchtown Island Cut to the Erne end of the Dernagore Cut, the navigation is largely through artificial cuts made to the north of the original Woodford River channel so that the latter, which is on the North/South border, forms three loops to the south of the navigation channel. These are in order of length Scotchtown, Dernagore and Cloncoohy, the last mentioned being quite the longest.

In between Scotchtown Island and Cloncoohy is Bray Wood, 'the finest and most extensive area of woodland along the canal'. There is a wet woodland flora at Scotchtown Island and similarly at places along all three of the old river channels. The EIS recommended that dredging in this area be performed with extreme care in order to protect the habitats.

The final area stretches — albeit discontinuously — from a point just upstream of Teemore Lough, along the outfall edge of Anoneen Lough and on to Upper Lough Erne. The most important features of this region are the fen communities around the two lakes and an area of reedswamp on the County Fermanagh side of the channel as it enters Upper Lough Erne.

Fish Examination of the fish population of the navigation showed that it is a good coarse fishery which is an important source of local revenue from the associated tourism. The principal fish present are Pike, Perch, Bream, Roach, Rudd, Hybrids and Gudgeon. While Brown Trout were found along the Woodford River system, they were numerous only at Ballyconnell.

Five spawning areas for Brown Trout were identified — at Corraquill [Caroul], at Ballyconnell, at Killarah and Callaghs [between Skelan and Bally-connell], between Coologe Lough and Skelan Lock [No 3], and between Ballyduff Bridge [No 18] and Ballyduff Lock [No 7]. Spawning areas for coarse fish were found mainly in the navigation channel: between Coologe and Derrycassan Loughs, between Derrycassan and Ballymagauran Loughs, and between St John's and Muckros Loughs, but also in the old river channel loop north of Carrickmakeegan Bridge [No 23]. In addition, the small lakes, Drumaleague Lough [west of the Letterfine Rock Cut and Lough Scur] and Lough Marrave [between Lough Scur and Castlefore Lock [No 8]], were considered important for natural restocking of the western part of the waterway.

Zoological Species Otters were not observed during the assessment but have been observed at Letterfine prior to the widening of the rock cut. However, they are known to live along the system, in particular, according to local information, between St John's Lough and Ballinamore.

Only one dragonfly was identified positively [*Aeschna grandis*] but at least one other [*Brachytron pratense*] is said to be found downstream of Aghalane. Damselfly species seen were: *Enallagma cyathigerum, Coenagrion puella, Ishnura elegans, Calopteryx virgo, Calopteryx splendens* and *Phyrrosoma nymphula*.

Common species of butterfly observed were: *Artogeia napi, Pieris brassicae, Pararge aegeria, Maniola jurtina* and *Vanessa atlanta*.

Ornithological Species The waterway is an important location for wintering wildfowl, in particular for the Whooper Swan, which breeds in Iceland, but also for dabbling and diving duck. While the studies made for the EIS were extensive they were not exhaustive and it was planned to carry out further counts of wintering wildfowl. However, the Whooper Swan was known to locate at Carrickmakeekan [near Bridge No 23], near either end of Ballymagauran Lough, and between Dernagore and Corraquill [Caroul]. Dabbling duck used locations at Carrickaport Lough [immediately west of Lough Scur], Lough Scur, St John's Lough, Garadice Lough [near the Haughton's Shore mooring] and Ballymagauran Lough. There were two breeding sites for Snipe, Curlew and Lapwing in County Fermanagh. A total of 21 areas along the canal was identified as being suitable for breeding waders.

Grey Wagtail were seen along the waterway system, and Dippers and Kingfishers were noted in some areas. There were Grasshopper Warblers at Ballymagauran Lough, while Reed Bunting and Sedge Warblers were found in the fen and carr areas. The lakes along the system had Great Crested Grebe, Mallard and both breeding and nonbreeding Mute Swans. According to local reports Teal and Tufted Duck both breed in the area of the waterway.

Landscape The EIS noted that 'the very limitations imposed on canal building by the need to keep a level water plane means that canals generally have a close fit with the topography and have a very happy relationship with the landscape. Even a large series of locks is unobtrusive, coinciding closely with the natural gradient of the land.'

The original construction had left a valuable legacy of very fine masonry structures — bridges, locks and wharves — whose stonework had survived remarkably well and which was in total harmony with the landscape. Of the bridges, the EIS aptly commented that 'these stone bridges were constructed with sensitivity and their refined sturdy appearance is a superb example of the stone-mason's craft. They span the canal in a most graceful manner, fit into the topography with dignity and have become important local landmarks.'

It was considered that the structures as a whole 'despite the years of decay and neglect still [had] charm' and that restoration would cause little change to the character of the canal and its surrounding landscape which had evolved without disruption from maintenance activities; the uninhibited growth along it formed a linear ribbon of landscape extending for miles in places.

Conservation Measures during Reconstruction

One of the most important factors to be considered was the effect of the water levels along the reconstructed navigation. It has been recounted that apart from the summit level at Lough Scur, where the summer navigation level would be restored to its original height of 67m [220ft] OD, and the reach from Castlefore, through St John's Lough, to Ballyduff, where the summer level would be raised by 0.7m [2.3ft] (and not to the original level), the water levels would be fixed at the existing mean summer levels — the levels which had evolved naturally over the years of dereliction and which had been adopted for use by both the human and wildlife populations along the waterway.

This approach would minimise disruption to spawning areas and to agriculture, and it would also maintain the existing drainage regime without inhibiting any future drainage activities. The main ecological effect of the raising of the level at the two reaches mentioned would be to increase the areas of littoral wetland habitats. The policy of no interference with sensitive areas already discussed, its essence being that neither removal nor disposal of spoil should be permitted on or along the banks in such areas. Also, as a general rule, the dredging or excavation of the channel would proceed in an upstream direction as this favoured the recolonisation of disturbed bottom areas by both plants and invertebrates.

Where spawning beds for Brown Trout were affected by excavation their reinstatement would only be carried out when such work was completed, lest gravel be covered by silt. If it were not practicable to replace the original gravel removed from spawning sites, natural gravel in an appropriate mix of sizes would be used. All the weirs on the Woodford River section of the navigation were found suitable for the provision of spawning gravels.

Other ecological protection measures would include the provision of nesting banks for Kingfishers along the steep south bank of the waterway between Ballyduff and Ballinamore, and the retention of some crevices in the stonework of the structures to provide nesting holes and ledges for Dippers and Grey Wagtails (which would also be provided with shallow stony habitats for feeding at channel margins).

As a final measure, all areas of woodland, hedgerows and scrubland to be retained would be protected from damage by machinery by being fenced off during the reconstruction.

Interested bodies consulted for EIS

Organisations in Ireland
An Taisce [Irish National Trust]
Ballinamore Angling and Tourism
  Association
Ballyconnell Angling and Tourism
  Association
Boat Hirers' Association
Bord Failte [Irish Tourist Board]
Cavan County Council
Central Fisheries Board (Northern
  Region)
Inland Waterways Association of
  Ireland
Irish Farmers' Association
Irish Wildbird Conservancy
Leitrim County Council
National Coarse Fishing Federation
Office of Public Works — Drainage
  Division
Office of Public Works — Wildlife
  Service
Teagasc [Agricultural Research
  Institute]
Organisations: Northern Ireland
Agricultural Producers' Assoc.
Cruise Hire Companies
Department of Agriculture
Department of the Environment —
  Countryside and Wildlife Branch
Fermanagh District Council
Fisheries Conservancy Board
National Trust
Northern Ireland Tourism Board
Royal Society for the Protection of
  Birds
Ulster Farmers' Union
Ulster Trust of Nature Conservation
Ulster Wildlife Trust
Other Organisations
British Tourist Authority
British Waterways Board
Commission of the European Union
European Tour Operators
European Travel Commission
French Tourist Authority
Netherlands Bureau voor Toerisme
World Tourism Organisation.

Table of the important Botanical Species

Area of Botanical Importance	Main Species of Importance
1. Upstream of Leitrim Village 400-900m from River Shannon	*Ranunculus lingua**; *Potamogeton alpinus**; *Sagittaria sagittifolia; Lemna trisulca.*
2. Entrance to Garadice Lough	*Lythrum portula.**
3. Woodford Lough to Ballymagauran Lough	Successional communities: fen-carr-woodland at Woodford Lough; and aquatic-reedswamp-fen-carr-wet heath and bog at south/ south-western end of Ballymagauran Lough. Also the EIS notes that 'the channel between these loughs holds a rich aquatic community by calcareous grassland, scrub and developing reedswamp.'
4. Scotchtown/ Cloncoohy/ Dernagore [old river channels]	Bray Wood consists principally of ash and hazel, with oak, elm and rowan. The understorey is of holly, blackthorn and bramble, with a rich ground flora. Flora at Scotchtown Island is dominated by alder and salix species. At Dernagore wetland flora includes *Cicuta virosa.*
5. Teemore Lough/ Anoneen Lough/ Upper Lough Erne	Fen communities dominated by *Carex acuta*, *Carex elata* and *Carex rostrata*; also *Osmunda regalis** and *Sagittaria sagittifolia*. Reedswamp dominated by flowering rush *Butomus umbellatus.*

* Not found elsewhere along the waterway

Water Levels at the areas of special Botanical Importance

Area of Botanical Importance	Water Level Regime Adopted
1. Upstream of Leitrim Village 400-900m from River Shannon	The water level would continue to be that of the Upper Shannon River at Leitrim.
2/3. Entrance to Garadice Lough and Woodford Lough to Ballymagauran Lough	The levels in the lakes, now to be controlled by the weir at Skelan [Kiltynaskellan] Lock [No 3], would remain unchanged as the height of the weir crest would be fixed at (i.e. reduced to) the present mean summer water level.
4. Scotchtown/ Cloncoohy /Dernagore [old river channels]	The height of the crest of the new weir at Corraquill [Caroul] Lock [No 1] would be fixed at the present mean summer level. This would be a reduction over the original weir height.
5. Teemore Lough/ Anonee Lough/ Upper Lough Erne	Water level would continue to be that of Upper Lough Erne.

CHAPTER 7

A DESCRIPTION OF THE NAVIGATION

A peculiarity of the navigation, the origins of which are unknown, was that the locks were numbered starting from the Erne, while the opposite was the case with the bridges, at least in the latter period. In the case of the locks, at least, their total has remained the same, but the reconstruction has seen a net reduction in the number of bridges. The navigation charts of the canal give definitive numberings of both locks and bridges and these are adhered to in the text below.

To avoid repetition, general descriptions are given below of the locks and bridges, individual details being presented in a gazetteer. As stated earlier, all eight locks on the Woodford River section are new, of reinforced concrete construction clad with masonry retrieved from the original locks, on the sites of which the replacements were built. The dimensions of the new locks are length 25m, width 6m, depth on cill 1.7m. To permit dredgers to travel throughout the river/lake section the width has been increased by 1m from the original dimension. The other eight locks, on the still-water canal section, have been repaired and rebuilt as necessary and retain their original dimensions of 25m x 5m x 1.7m. The deepest lock is that at Castlefore, which has a rise of over 4m. At each lock there are concrete moorings upstream and downstream, to permit crews easy access to the lock controls. There are also canoe landings. All locks (and mooring locations have attractive nameboards.

All locks have steel gates, some with galvanized steel footboards, some without, but all having timber heel and mitre posts and cill beams. They are electro-hydraulically operated from a control panel mounted on a pillar midway along the top of each lock. Full instructions are given on the faceplate of the control panels as well, of course, as in the navigational guide. To prevent gates being closed while being obstructed by a boat there are protective sensors which must be unimpeded before lock operation is possible.

Should boats be too close to moving gates or be foul of the lock cill a warning siren sounds. Also, when a lock is in use approaching boats from either direction are controlled by traffic signals. Should problems arise each panel has an overriding emergency stop button as well as a call button for assistance, via radio link, from the ranger in the nearest waterway control centre.

As a result of this automation there are neither lock houses nor lock keepers on the reconstructed navigation. Operations are the responsibility of the boat users, who gain access to the lock controls by means of a magnetized plastic card — a 'smart card' — which may be obtained from any shop bearing the distinctive logo of the canal. [The same outlets also have available tokens which, either separately or in combination with the lock cards, provide access to the utilities and services along the waterway.] This user-friendly system will undoubtedly add to the pleasure of negotiating the navigation, not least because it affords the maximum degree of freedom to boat crews to sail or moor at wil between the official opening hours — 09.00 to 20.00.

The waterway now has a total of twelve weirs, four of which are relatively small overflows [parallel to the navigation channel] for the discharge of surplus water at Locks 13-16 on the still-water section, and eight of which are more substantial ones either straight across or at an angle to the channel at Locks 1-8 along the Woodford River section. All are fixed weirs, bar one, constructed of reinforced concrete, and protected either by a fixed barrier [at Lock 1] or by a galvanized steel walkway which permits crossing of the navigation [Locks 2-7]. The exception is the weir at Castlefore [Lock 8], at the eastern end of the summit level, where there is a regulating sluice.

All the original masonry bridges have been retained, again with one exception, after underpinning and repairs as appropriate. The exception is the bridge at Aghalane, the bridge nearest the Erne. This was destroyed in an explosion in the early 1970s and has not been replaced. Apart from a few extra accommodation bridges, some of which were unauthorized additions to the original works, and two old iron railway bridges, the remaining bridges at the start of reconstruction were concrete structures, often unlovely and very basic, which afforded inadequate headroom. These have largely been replaced by new concrete bridges which have been clad with masonry in order to harmonize with the overall ambience of the canal; in a minority of cases bridges were retained but with raised decks. Finally, there is one new steel footbridge which replaces a post-Award accommodation bridge.

MAPS and GAZETTEER

Photo: April 1994, Frank Miller, The Irish Times

Maps

THE RIVER SHANNON

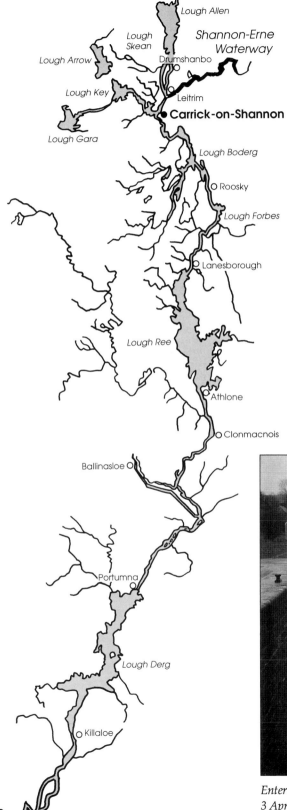

Lough Allen

Lough Skean

Shannon-Erne Waterway

Lough Arrow

Drumshanbo

Lough Key

Leitrim

Carrick-on-Shannon

Lough Gara

Lough Boderg

O Roosky

Lough Forbes

O Lanesborough

Lough Ree

Athlone

O Clonmacnois

Ballinasloe O

Portumna

Lough Derg

Killaloe

Limerick

*Entering Lock No. 9, bound for the Erne,
3 April 1994.*

LEITRIM TO MUCKROS LOUGH

MAP 1

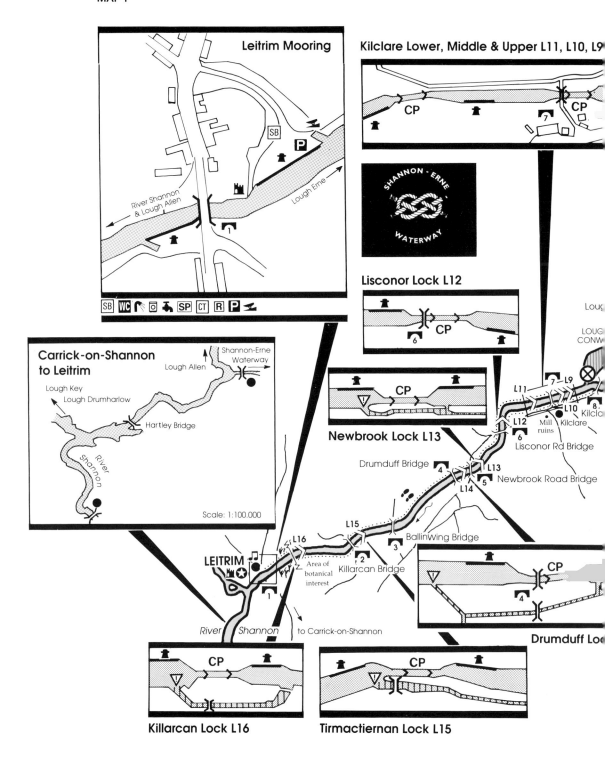

Leitrim Mooring

River Shannon & Lough Allen

Lough Erne

SB

P

Kilclare Lower, Middle & Upper L11, L10, L9

CP

CP

7

SHANNON · ERNE WATERWAY

Lisconor Lock L12

CP

6

Carrick-on-Shannon to Leitrim

Shannon-Erne Waterway

Lough Allen

Lough Key

Lough Drumharlow

Hartley Bridge

River Shannon

Scale: 1:100.000

Newbrook Lock L13

CP

Drumduff Bridge

L11

L9

7

L10

8.

Kilcla

L12

Mill ruins

Kilclare

6

Lisconor Rd Bridge

L13

5

Newbrook Road Bridge

L14

4

Drumduff Lo

CP

L15

L16

LEITRIM

Area of botanical interest

Killarcan Bridge

2

3

Ballinwing Bridge

1

River Shannon

to Carrick-on-Shannon

CP

CP

Killarcan Lock L16

Tirmactiernan Lock L15

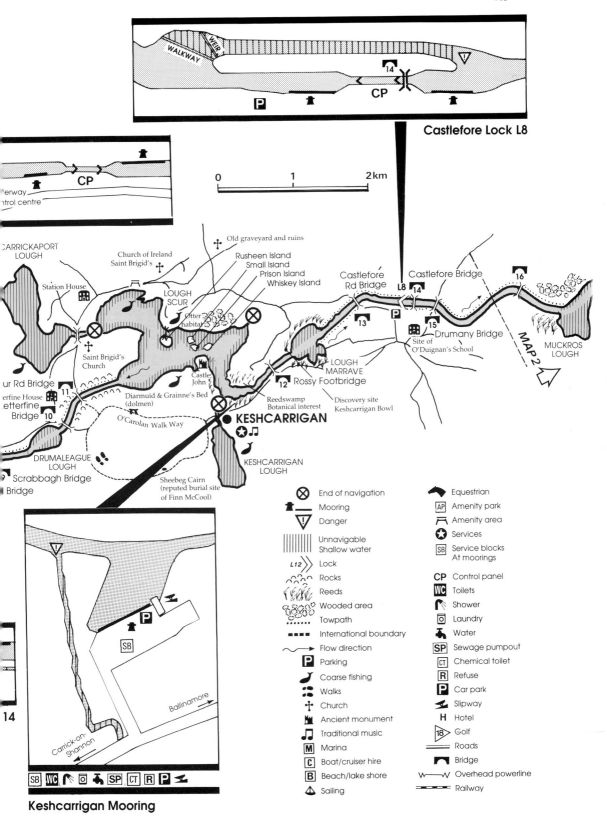

Castlefore Lock L8

Keshcarrigan Mooring

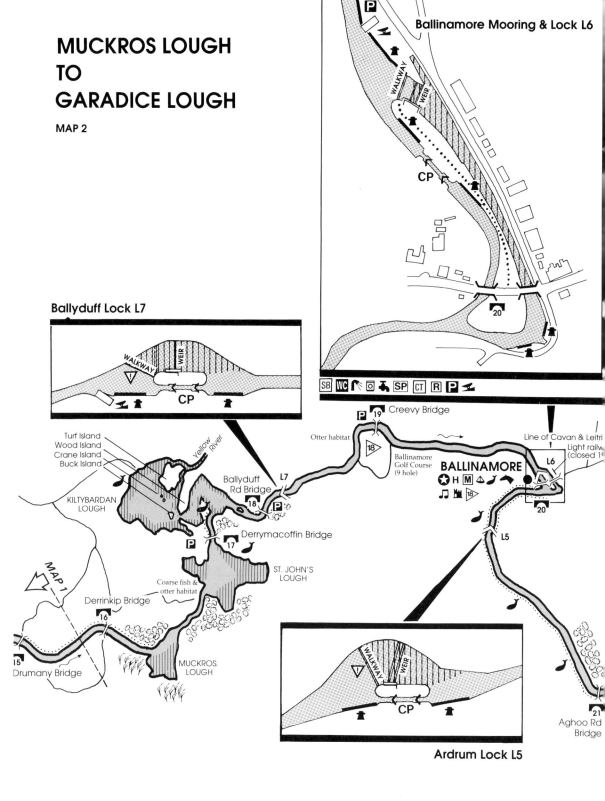

MUCKROS LOUGH
TO
GARADICE LOUGH

MAP 2

To golf course

Ballinamore Mooring & Lock L6

WALKWAY

WEIR

CP

20

Ballyduff Lock L7

WALKWAY

WEIR

CP

SB WC ○ ⬛ SP CT R P

P 19 Creevy Bridge

Otter habitat

18

Ballinamore
Golf Course
(9 hole)

Line of Cavan & Leitri

Light railw
(closed 1

L6

BALLINAMORE

★ H M ⬛

♫ 18

20

Turf Island
Wood Island
Crane Island
Buck Island

Yellow River

Ballyduff
Rd Bridge

L7

18

P

KILTYBARDAN
LOUGH

L5

Derrymacoffin Bridge

17

P

ST. JOHN'S
LOUGH

MAP 1

Coarse fish &
otter habitat

Derrinkip Bridge

16

15

Drumany Bridge

MUCKROS
LOUGH

WALKWAY

WEIR

CP

21

Aghoo Rd
Bridge

Ardrum Lock L5

SHANNON - ERNE WATERWAY

⊗	End of navigation	⮲	Equestrian
⚓	Mooring	AP	Amenity park
▽	Danger	⛩	Amenity area
‖‖‖	Unnavigable Shallow water	✪	Services
L12 ⟩⟩	Lock	SB	Service blocks At moorings
	Rocks	CP	Control panel
	Reeds	WC	Toilets
	Wooded area		Shower
⋯⋯	Towpath	⊡	Laundry
▬▬	International boundary		Water
⟿	Flow direction	SP	Sewage pumpout
P	Parking	CT	Chemical toilet
	Coarse fishing	R	Refuse
	Walks	P	Car park
✝	Church		Slipway
	Ancient monument	H	Hotel
♫	Traditional music	18⟩	Golf
M	Marina	══	Roads
C	Boat/cruiser hire		Bridge
B	Beach/lake shoe	⌇	Overhead powerline
⛵	Sailing	▬▬	Railway

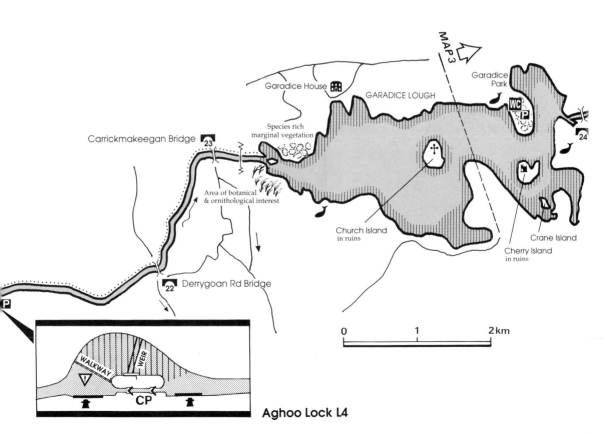

MAP 3

Garadice House

GARADICE LOUGH

Garadice Park

WC
P

Carrickmakeegan Bridge 23

Species rich marginal vegetation

24

Area of botanical & ornithological interest

Church Island
in ruins

Crane Island

Cherry Island
in ruins

Derrygoan Rd Bridge
22

P

| 0 | 1 | 2km |

WALKWAY WEIR

CP

Aghoo Lock L4

GARADICE LOUGH TO BALLYCONNELL

MAP 3

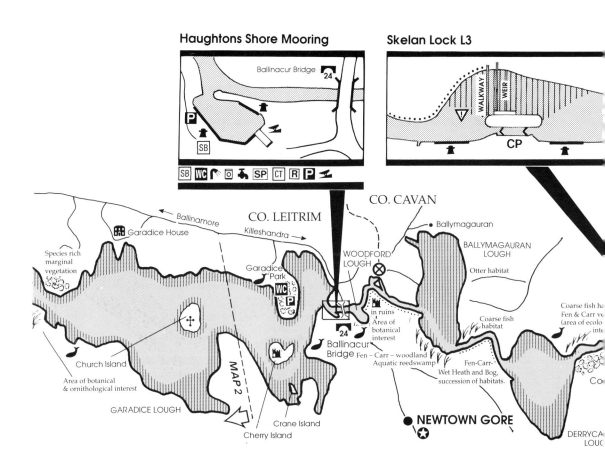

Haughtons Shore Mooring

Ballinacur Bridge 24

P
SB

SB WC ⌂ ▢ ♁ SP CT R P ⤢

Skelan Lock L3

WALKWAY
WEIR
CP

CO. CAVAN

Ballinamore ←
Killeshandra →

CO. LEITRIM

Garadice House

Species rich
marginal
vegetation

Garadice
Park

WC
P

Church Island

Area of botanical
& ornithological interest

GARADICE LOUGH

MAP 2

Crane Island
Cherry Island

WOODFORD
LOUGH

Ballinacur
Bridge

24

in ruins
Area of
botanical
interest

Fen – Carr – woodland
Aquatic reedswamp

Ballymagauran

BALLYMAGAURAN
LOUGH

Otter habitat

Coarse fish
habitat

Coarse fish ha
Fen & Carr ve
(area of ecolo
inte

Fen-Carr-
Wet Heath and Bog,
succession of habitats.

Co

● NEWTOWN GORE
✪

DERRYCA
LOU

⊗ End of navigation		∿→ Flow direction		⤢ Equestrian	
⚓ Mooring		P Parking		AP Amenity park	
▽! Danger		♁ Coarse fishing		⊼ Amenity area	
‖‖‖ Unnavigable Shallow water		⁚⁚ Walks		✪ Services	
L12 》 Lock		✝ Church		SB Service blocks At moorings	
∿ Rocks		♫ Traditional music		CP Control panel	
𝒲 Reeds		M Marina		WC Toilets	
⚬ Wooded area		C Boat/cruiser hire		⌂ Shower	
⋯⋯ Towpath		B Beach/lake shore		▢ Laundry	
▪▪▪ International boundary		△ Sailing		♁ Water	

Ballyconnell Mooring

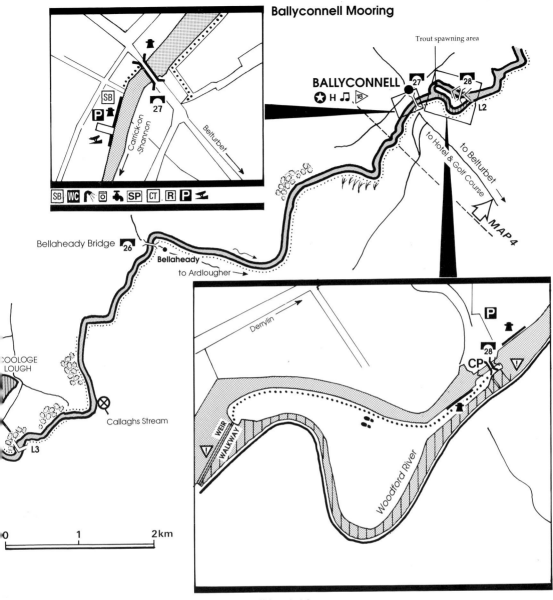

Trout spawning area

BALLYCONNELL

27

28

L2

to Hotel & Golf Course

to Belturbet

MAP 4

Bellaheady Bridge 26

Bellaheady

to Ardlougher →

COOLOGE LOUGH

Callaghs Stream

L3

Carrick-on-Shannon

Belturbet →

SB

27

SB WC O SP CT R P

Ballyconnell Lock L2

Derrylin

WEIR

WALKWAY

Woodford River

CP

28

0   1   2km

SP Sewage pumpout
CT Chemical toilet
R   Refuse
P   Car park
    Slipway
H   Hotel
18 Golf
=   Roads
    Bridge
W   Overhead powerline
    Railway

SHANNON - ERNE WATERWAY

BALLYCONNELL TO LOWER LOUGH ERNE

MAP 4

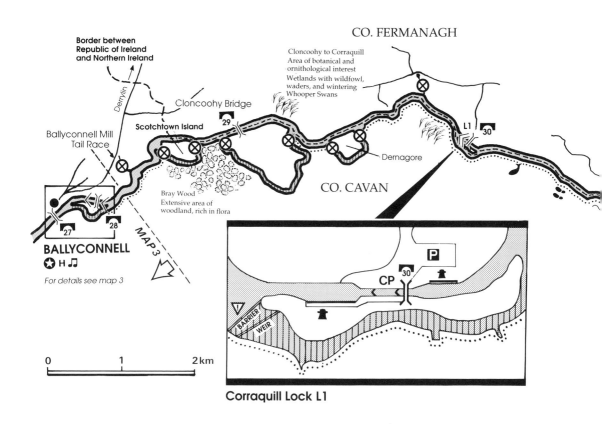

CO. FERMANAGH

Border between
Republic of Ireland
and Northern Ireland

Derrylin

Cloncoohy to Corraquill
Area of botanical and
ornithological interest

Wetlands with wildfowl,
waders, and wintering
Whooper Swans

Cloncoohy Bridge

Scotchtown Island

29

Ballyconnell Mill
Tail Race

Dernagore

L1 30

Bray Wood
Extensive area of
woodland, rich in flora

CO. CAVAN

27 28

BALLYCONNELL
✪ H ♫

For details see map 3

MAP3

0   1   2 km

Corraquill Lock L1

CP 30 P

BARRIER WEIR

⊗ End of navigation	∿→ Flow direction	🐴 Equestrian	SP Sewage pumpout
⚓ Mooring	P Parking	AP Amenity park	CT Chemical toilet
▽! Danger	♪ Coarse fishing	📐 Amenity area	R Refuse
‖‖‖ Unnavigable Shallow water	👣 Walks	✪ Services	P Car park
L12 〉 Lock	✝ Church	SB Service blocks At moorings	⚓ Slipway
⌇ Rocks	🎵 Ancient monument	CP Control panel	H Hotel
🌿 Reeds	♫ Traditional music	WC Toilets	18〉 Golf
🌳 Wooded area	M Marina	🚿 Shower	Roads
⋯⋯ Towpath	C Boat/cruiser hire	▣ Laundry	⌐ Bridge
▪▪▪ International boundary	B Beach/lake shore	♣ Water	W—W Overhead powerline
	⛵ Sailing		▭ Railway

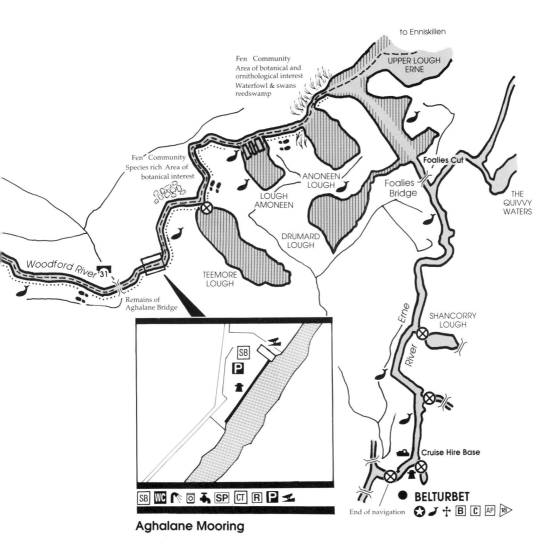

to Enniskillen

UPPER LOUGH ERNE

Fen Community
Area of botanical and
ornithological interest
Waterfowl & swans
reedswamp

Foalies Cut

Fen Community
Species rich Area of
botanical interest

ANONEEN
LOUGH

Foalies
Bridge

THE
QUIVVY
WATERS

LOUGH
AMONEEN

DRUMARD
LOUGH

Woodford River 31

TEEMORE
LOUGH

Remains of
Aghalane Bridge

SHANCORRY
LOUGH

Erne

River

SB
P

Cruise Hire Base

BELTURBET

SB WC O SP CT R P

Aghalane Mooring

End of navigation

SHANNON - ERNE WATERWAY

UPPER & LOWER LOUGH ERNE

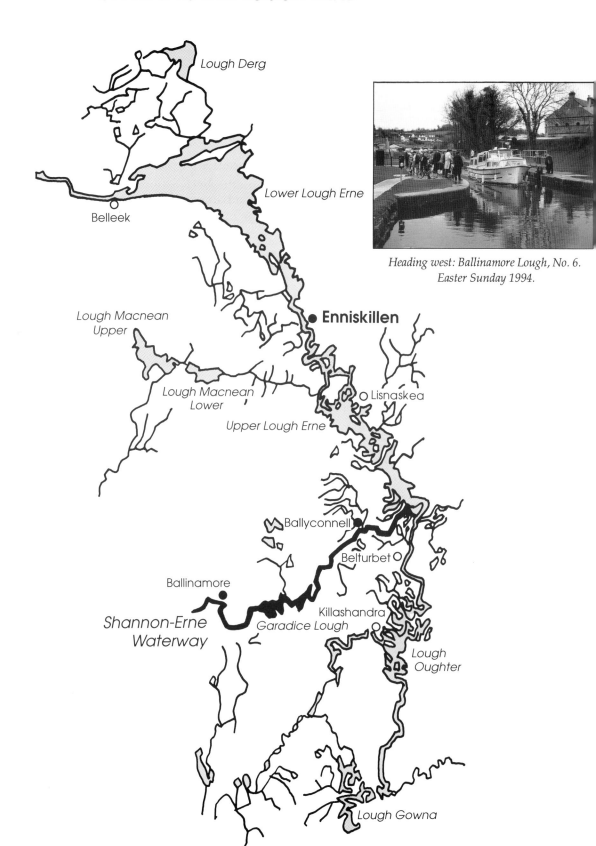

Lough Derg

Belleek

Lower Lough Erne

● **Enniskillen**

*Lough Macnean
Upper*

*Lough Macnean
Lower*

○ Lisnaskea

Upper Lough Erne

Ballyconnell

Belturbet ○

Ballinamore

*Shannon-Erne
Waterway*

Killashandra ○

Garadice Lough

*Lough
Oughter*

Lough Gowna

*Heading west: Ballinamore Lough, No. 6.
Easter Sunday 1994.*

THE GAZETTEER

The text below is presented in a quick-reference gazetteer format so that the salient details, and a capsule history of the many features along the navigation, may be easily found. The designations RH [right-hand side] and LH [left-hand side] are used as appropriate for the traveller from the Shannon to the Erne. Where appropriate, features are described as being at the 'east' [Erne] end or 'west' [Shannon] end even though this may be directionally inaccurate at times. Bridges are designated 'Road' or 'Accommodation' in accordance with the 1860 Awards or, in the case of additional structures, their function.

A great benefit of the reconstruction of the navigation is the virtual total accessibility of the different sites mentioned below. Apart from Lock No 1, at Corraquill in County Fermanagh, which must be approached from the LH [northern side], each location may be visited from either side of the waterway, and access may be gained to either side of the channel.

The details given below are intended to be comprehensive but it is very important to note that they do not constitute directions for navigation. No gazetteer can ever take the place of the excellent 'Navigational Guide to the Shannon-Erne Waterway', which contains the official navigation charts on which are shown the exact locations of channel markers and of all features along the waterway. This guide, which incorporates clear navigational instructions as well as full details of how to use the locks and other facilities [in three languages] is an essential requirement both for the traveller along the canal and for the general enthusiast.

It should be noted that, as in rural Ireland the townland name is the invariable local area designator, this practice of using the appropriate townland names has been adopted for the designation of the features along the reconstructed waterway. However, in the past there was often a great deal of confusion over nomenclature as the navigation in many places constituted the mearing between townlands, and so two or more names might be equally applicable to a given point. Alternatively, a single name could legitimately be applied to two or more distinct features — for example, Locks Nos 9/10/11 have all at times been referred to as Kilclare. Wisely, the policy of giving each lock a distinctive name has been adopted (with only rare exceptions) and the designations below are in accordance with this. In those cases where alternative names were in common usage, either locally or in official documents, such names are given below in brackets after the current official name.

All distances are given in kilometres [km; 1km = 0.625 mile], from and to the official commencement and termination points of the waterway. The open figures are for distances from the Shannon at Leitrim; those in brackets are calculated from Upper Lough Erne.

Km

00.00   Junction with the River Shannon — Commencement of the
[63.40] Navigation. The Shannon-Erne waterway is to the right; bearing left
         at the junction leads to Battle Bridge, a short distance upstream. [The
         latter is the 'End of Navigation' on the Shannon proper, but a lock
         [RH/east] marks the entrance to the Lough Allen Canal, restored by
         the OPW, which leads via Acres Lough to Lough Allen, the
         northernmost of the three major lakes on the River Shannon.]

00.32   Leitrim Moorings and Bridge: No 1. The bridge here was built in
[63.08] 1849-50 and has a single masonry arch. Just before it is the old wharf
         [RH], complete with stone mooring posts; it was built in 1850. By 1970
         it had been provided with electric lighting, a drinking water tap, and
         picnic table for boats coming in off the Shannon. Even though it was
         virtually the limit of navigation on the derelict waterway it was a
         pleasant and popular mooring, despite its limited accommodation for
         boats. The bridge carries the road from Carrick-on-Shannon to
         Drumshanbo and on through North Leitrim to Donegal.

         A little past the bridge [LH] is a public mooring, immediately beyond
         which is a turning area for boats; the floating mooring is a new facility,
         built to accommodate variations in the Shannon water level and to
         complement the old wharf. It has an attractive masonry Service Block
         building, available to boating visitors, housing toilets, shower and
         laundry facilities. There are also sewage pumpout facilities.

00.80   Black Lough [Site]. This was originally a small lake situated in the
[62.60] swampy region between Killarcan Lock and Leitrim Bridge. The lake
         itself became part of the original waterway, but its legacy is the area
         of botanical interest on either bank of the navigation just west of
         Killarcan Lock [No 16].

00.95   Killarcan [Leitrim] Lock: No 16. This is the first of the 8 locks in the
[62.45] still-water canal section, all of which were built between 1849 and
         1851. It is sometimes referred to as 'Leitrim Lock', because of its
         proximity to Leitrim village. Immediately to the right of the original
         lock stood the first toll collector's house, built in 1857. The house was
         still extant, though in a very ruinous state, until the reconstruction; it
         had been inhabited until the 1950s. It was a substantial two-storey
         stone structure with a yard, enclosed by a stone wall, at the back [west
         end]. A distinguishing feature of the house, a consequence of its bleak
         elevated site and complete lack of protection from south-westerly

storms, was the back wall which was completely blank, apart from one small window. Unfortunately, the house, which would have been a most distinctive memorial to the old navigation, had to be demolished because of its state and its location which would have been a hindrance to those using the new waterway. Above the lock there is an upstream [RH] overflow weir which diverts excess water around the lock chamber. This lock was underpinned and altered as a consequence of the lowering of the channel bed from Lock No 15. The chamber is a magnificent inverted masonry arch. Below this lock (and Nos 9-15) is a small pumphouse used when necessary to augment the summit level water supply.

01.70   Killarcan Accommodation Bridge: No 2. Less than 100 metres before
[61.70]   Lock No 15 is this masonry arch bridge, originally built in 1850. The bridge has been underpinned, improved and repaired. Below the bridge was originally an overflow by which surplus water flowed from the canal into a drain which ran through Tirmactiernan and Carrickaveril townlands to a swampy region, formerly the Black Lough [see above], where it again entered the canal, below Lock No 16. A maze of channels was dug as part of the drainage district here, to the right of the waterway.

01.82   Tirmactiernan [Killarcan] Lock: No 15. Just above the lock [RH] is
[61.58]   quite a large overflow weir by which surplus water is channelled past the lock chamber, to re-enter just below. In the reconstruction this lock was underpinned and made deeper to permit the lowering of the level to Lock No 16.

02.31   Ballinwing [Sheffield] Accommodation Bridge: No 3. This is a single
[61.09]   masonry arch dating from 1849. It is referred to as 'Crossycarwill Bridge' on Ordnance Survey maps.

03.41   Drumduff [Sheffield] Lock: No 14, and Accommodation Bridge: No
[59.99]   4. The latter was built across the west end of the lock in 1859, for John Kane. It was replaced in 1926 by a simple concrete structure. The current bridge is a new structure, a vast improvement; it is similar to No 7 and other bridges. An overflow drain leaves the canal by weir above the lock [RH] rejoining again downstream. The old alternative name is that of an adjoining townland.

03.63   Newbrook Road Bridge: No 5. Built in 1849-50 this is a fine stone
[59.77]   structure with a skew arch. It carries the Carrick-on-Shannon /Ballinamore road.

03.80   Newbrook Lock: No 13. This is a deep lock with an overflow weir and
[59.60]   drain for surplus water. It leaves the channel above the lock [RH] and rejoins just below.

04.40   Lisconor Lock: No 12 & Lisconor Road Bridge: No 6. Immediately
[59.00] beyond the bridge is the lock, to the left of which originally was a lock
house, long disappeared. This, however, did not have a resident lock
keeper for long and its history is something of a minor mystery; it was
built in 1857. The bridge, on the road from Carrick-on-Shannon to
Ballinamore, is a slightly skewed masonry arch erected in 1849-50.

05.19   Kilclare Lower [Kilclarebeg] Lock: No 11. As the levels from this Lock
[58.21] to the next [No 10] and from the latter to No 9 are quite short, and
temporary water shortages may result in the levels depending on lock
usage, water level gauge indicators have been provided at all three
locks to show the exact situation to boat crews. When the levels are
found to be insufficient, crews should contact the control centre by
means of the call button on the control panel; the ranger in charge will
rectify the position, by controlled pumping.

05.39   Kilclare Middle [Drumruekill] Lock: No 10, and Accommodation
[58.01] Bridge: No 7. The original bridge, across the lower end of the lock,
was provided 'for Mr King's tenants' in 1857. By the early 1970s it
comprised a simple concrete structure which has been replaced by a
new bridge. This lock is the site of a Waterway Control Centre; it is
housed [RH] in a fine masonry building similar to the Service Blocks.
Another minor, but pleasing, feature is the preserved remnant of Pat
Doherty's Kilclare cornmill [RH].

Across the Summit Level

05.59   [Kilclaremore] Lock: No 9. [Start of Summit Level] Boats bound for
[57.81] the Shannon must only proceed when there is adequate water, as
indicated by the water level indicators [cf entry under Lock No 11
above].

05.83   Lough Conway Outfall [LH]. This is marked by an 'End of
[57.57] Navigation' sign.

06.00   Kilclare Road Bridge: No 8. This is a very fine stone bridge, comprising
[57.40] a single skew arch [RH]. Built in 1849-50, it carries the
Carrick-on-Shannon/Ballinamore road.

06.34   Scrabbagh Accommodation Bridge: No 9. Built in 1850, this consists
[57.06] of a single masonry arch with a narrow roadway.

07.09   Drumaleague Lough [Entry]. A short distance past Bridge No 9 a
[56.31] marked channel leads through this small lake.

07.26   Drumaleague Lough [Exit]/Letterfine Rock Cutting [Start]. This, the
[56.14] principal feature of the original canal in engineering terms, merits a
special note. It is a deep cutting through the limestone which runs

from Drumaleague Lough to Lough Scur. Originally 8m wide it has been widened to 15m so that boats may pass freely without the need for a 'single-lane' system.

07.49   Letterfine Road Bridge: No 10. This is a one-arch masonry bridge built
[55.91]   in 1852 across the rock cutting. It carries a minor alternative road from
          Keshcarrigan to Drumshanbo.

07.88   Lough Scur Road Bridge: No 11. This carries the county road from
[55.52]   Keshcarrigan to Drumshanbo; it is a single masonry arch erected in
          1852 and it crosses the rock cutting, almost exactly at its mid-point.

08.50   Lough Scur [Entry]. A pair of channel markers, a little into the lake,
[54.90]   may be regarded as the entrance to Lough Scur, a very pleasant
          though small lake which is the central point of the summit level. It is
          fed by the diverted Kiltubrid [Driny] and Aghacashlaun Rivers. It had
          navigation markers originally and again has a marked channel
          leading roughly eastwards towards the small Whiskey Island. The
          greater part of the lake may be explored by water, the charts showing
          'End of Navigation' signs at the cut to Carrickaport Lough, near
          Drumcong, and at the inflow, at Driny, of the Aghacashlaun River.

An interesting point of note is that a little to the southeast of Whiskey Island (at the end of the entry marker series from the Keshcarrigan direction), at a point opposite the ruins of Castle John, the style of the markers changes. Thus far they have been of the pattern standard on the Shannon system; here, halfway along the summit level, they change to the Erne pattern. Both styles are described in the 'Navigational Guide', which is recommended here.

The reason for the generous provision of navigation markers in this vicinity is that the reconstruction involved the restoration of a depth for navigation in the summit level. This involved, especially around Lough Scur, the submerging of much, largely sloping, land which had become exposed (and thus in effect available for tillage) when the retaining lock gates of the original navigation crumbled away. Accordingly, in the shallow area to the eastern part of Lough Scur, there is only an adequate depth for boats in the navigation channel proper, hence the careful marking.

10.31   Lough Scur [Exit]. An 'End of Navigation' sign [RH] marks the outlet
[53.09]   of a stream from Keshcarrigan Lough, at a point which may be
          regarded as the exit from the lake.

10.54   Keshcarrigan Mooring [Harbour] [RH]. Situated about 1 km east of
[52.86]   Keshcarrigan village, this is another completely new feature. There is
          a long quay, a launching slip and sewage pumpout facility. Toilet,
          shower and laundry facilities are provided in the standard Service

Block building. The location is roughly mid-way between the Shannon and Ballinamore and is well placed for those who have traversed or who are about to travel the still-water canal with its eight locks. The village has shops and pubs, offering entertainment.

11.07 Rossy Footbridge: No 12. This arched, steel accommodation
[52.33] footbridge is a distinctive new replacement structure for an earlier — though not original — bridge of a very basic nature.

11.41 Lough Marrave [Entry]. This is a small lake with a straight marked
[51.99] course through it.

11.69 Lough Marrave [Exit].
[51.71]

12.52 Castlefore Road Bridge: No 13. This masonry bridge, with a single
[50.88] skew arch, built in 1851-2, is on a minor road from Castlefore to Annadale. It is in the townland of Kilmacsherwell.

13.22 Castlefore Lock: No 8, and Accommodation Bridge: No 14. [End of
[50.18] Summit Level]. The channel divides, navigation to the right, where it enters a channel leading to the lock originally designed with a lift of 4.1 metres; it was built in 1853-4. Opposite the lock [RH] was a lock house built in 1857; it has long since disappeared. At the east end of the reconstructed lock is a new accommodation bridge similar to that at Ballyconnell and like it an additional rather than a replacement structure. A pumping station east of the lock [RH] has been provided to augment the supply in the summit level in dry seasons.

The left-hand channel runs to the weir, near the point where the Aghacashlaun River used to flow in before its diversion into Lough Scur in the 1840s scheme. The original 30.5m long weir was built in 1852-3. The new weir is fitted with a sluice, the only one on the reconstructed river navigation section.

The River Navigation: Castlefore-Ballinamore

13.58 Drumany Accommodation Bridge: No 15. This bridge was built in
[49.82] 1849; it was one of the most interesting, being the only wrought iron lattice girder structure, at least in later years. It was narrow and rested on masonry abutments. It has been replaced by a new concrete masonry clad bridge; it carries a very minor road.

14.89 Derrinkip [Muckros] Accommodation Bridge: No 16. A wooden
[48.51] bridge was built in 1855 and replaced in 1876. The bridge in 1970 was a more recent structure, consisting of a single narrow concrete span. The current bridge is new and carries a very minor road.

15.52 Muckros Lough [Entry]. The channel curves roughly north-east along
[47.88] the northern end of this small lake.

16.45 Muckros Lough [Exit].
[46.95]

16.55 Muckros Accommodation Bridge [Site]. A latter-day additional
[46.85] concrete structure ['Ferry Bridge'] was located in the narrows
between St John's and Muckros Loughs. It was removed and not
replaced in the reconstruction.

16.63 St John's Lough [Entry]. This was provided with navigation markers
[46.77] in 1857-8, and again in 1993, at entry and exit.

17.33 St John's Lough [Exit]. The navigation leaves St John's Lough proper.
[46.07]

17.50 Derrymacoffin Accommodation Bridge: No 17. A 10.5m span bridge
[45.90] was built here across narrows in the St John's Lough system in 1854-5.
A replacement bridge was provided in 1932; it collapsed in 1948 as
two men and a horse and cart were crossing. A fairly primitive
replacement concrete structure was put up shortly afterwards. This
has now been replaced by a high single span. The roadway to
Derrymacoffin is a cul-de-sac, the bridge being at its end, where there
is a parking area, principally for anglers.

17.76 Entry to Lower [Northern] Lake in St John's Lough System.
[45.64]

18.12 Exit from St John's Lough System. The navigation course is to the
[45.28] right, just past Derrymacoffin Bridge, via a well marked channel
which makes a virtual U-turn here to enter a narrow passage leading
on to Ballyduff. However, as an adjunct to the reconstruction work,
another well-marked channel, to the left, has been provided between
Wood Island and Buck Island, leading into Kiltybardan Lough, a
recreational water off the main navigation, into which the Yellow
River was diverted in the original scheme. Reference to the
'Navigational Guide' by boat users is recommended.

18.63 Ballyduff Road Bridge: No 18. This is a single arch masonry bridge,
[44.77] built in 1849-50; it is on the Ballinamore-Drumshanbo road.

19.00 Ballyduff Lock: No 7. At this point, lock, sluice, fish pass and weir
[44.40] originally stretched across the channel, right to left. The lock was built
in 1853-4. The old weir, 3.35m high and 30.5m long (with a dog-leg
along it) was built in 1854. As at Skelan, flash boards were fitted to
this weir [to raise the level back to Castlefore]. There was no lock
house. Prior to reconstruction the site was virtually impenetrable with
overgrowth. It is now an attractive open location with weir [LH], fish
pass and lock [RH] spanning the river. There is a boat slipway [RH].

19.87   Yellow River [Old Course] Outfall [LH]. As part of the original works
[43.53] the river was diverted into Kiltybardan Lough, part of the St John's
        Lough system.

20.70   Ballinamore Golf Course/Creevy Bridge: No 19. The accommodation
[42.70] bridge is a new structure, replacing one erected some 30 years
        previously, and providing access across the navigation to the 9-hole
        golf course [RH]. The narrow road on the left which is above but
        parallel to the canal from Ballyduff to Ballinamore is quite new, being
        the course of the non-roadside section of the Arigna Tramway section
        of the Cavan & Leitrim Railway, opened in 1888 and closed in 1959.

21.39   Castlerogy River Outfall [LH]. Entry of a small tributary.
[42.01]

22.70   Ballinamore Quay. Where originally there were no facilities at all, and
[40.70] more recently a fairly impenetrable jungle, there are now extensive
        facilities which befit Ballinamore as the central focal point of the new
        waterway. These include a slipway, Service Block, and generous
        moorings. There is a very pleasant expanse of water here. Ballinamore
        is the administrative headquarters of the Shannon-Erne Waterway
        Ltd. A full range of services is provided.

22.84   Ballinamore Lock: No 6. Originally dating from 1849-50, the lock is a
[40.56] short distance above the bridge. Adjacent to the lock, on the left were,
        in order, large sluice, fish pass and weir; these have been replaced by
        the new weir, fish pass and walkway.

23.01   Ballinamore Navigation Road Bridge: No 20. The navigation channel
[40.39] bears to the right past the lock, and runs under a single arch stone
        bridge [built 1848-49]. On the northern side of the roadway between
        the navigation and river bridges was the lock house, built in 1857.
        Now demolished it was inhabited up to relatively recent years. A
        point of interest is that its original occupant, lock keeper Michael
        Ferguson, was still in residence in 1888 when the railway line to
        Arigna opened, and was recommended for the job of tending the
        adjacent Lower Town Gates [level crossing] at the sum of 2 shillings
        [10p] a week.

23.05   Ballinamore River Bridge and Wharf [Site] [LH]. The river channel, to
[40.35] the left of the lock, and crossed by a walkway connecting the moorings
        to the lock island, runs under a 3-arch masonry bridge, not one of the
        formal structures of the old navigation. Prior to the building of the
        Arigna branch of the Cavan & Leitrim Railway in 1887-8 there was a
        wharf [LH] just beyond the bridge — similar to that at Leitrim, and
        was conveniently placed near the Market House [1847-1971], which
        was east of it. The railway works were built on the wharf site and they

also obliterated the fourth arch of the river bridge. The Fohera River joins the canal in this 'basin', as it is known. There are two new concrete moorings near which is a bilingually inscribed limestone boulder similar to one at Ballyconnell. It marks the visit to Ballinamore of An Taoiseach, Mr C.J. Haughey, on 26. 11. 1990 to inaugurate the restoration project. The distance quoted is for the junction.

The River Navigation: Ardrum-Ballyconnell

23.90 Ardrum Lock: No 5. Features here were and are virtually identical to
[39.50] those at Aghoo and Kiltynaskellan [see below], and their arrangement was the same — lock, sluice, fish pass and weir across the channel. The lock was built in 1851-2 and the old 46m weir was built in 1852. There was no lock house. Although quite close to Ballinamore this site, being in a valley well below the parallel road, was quite inaccessible, remaining thus until the reconstruction.

25.31 Aghoo West: Cavan & Leitrim Railway Bridge [Site]. Here, a low
[38.09] lattice-girder iron bridge without headroom carried the Dromod-Ballinamore line of the narrow-gauge Cavan & Leitrim Railway [1887-1959] across the waterway. It was abandoned on closure of the line, only being cleared away in the reconstruction.

26.39 Aghoo Road Bridge: No 21. This is a single-span masonry bridge,
[37.01] 10.5m span by 6.4m roadway, built in 1852-3. It carries the road from Ballinamore to Cloone but is just north of Aghoo Cross which gives access to Fenagh and Carrigallen.

26.82 Aghoo Lock: No 4. Here originally were a lock, sluice, fish pass and
[36.58] 39m weir. The lock was built in 1854-5, and parallel to it was an 1857 lock house, long a memory. As elsewhere on the new waterway a galvanized steel walkway across the river channel provides easy access from the bank opposite the lock, which is to the right.

28.38 Lisnatullagh Accommodation Bridge [Site]. A wooden
[35.02] accommodation bridge with a 2.5m roadway was erected in 1857. By 1970 the structure was an extremely ramshackle timber affair, supported by a central concrete pier and offering no headroom. During the reconstruction commonsense prevailed among all interested parties and the offending structure was removed without replacement.

28.86 Derrygoan Road Bridge: No 22. A wooden 10.5m span bridge, with a
[34.54] 3.5m roadway and giving 4m headroom, was built in 1855. It was replaced by a concrete structure about 1920. This has now been superseded by a new bridge. It carries a minor public road from Aghyowla.

30.70 Carrickmakeegan Accommodation Bridge: No 23. This was originally
[32.70] a wooden accommodation bridge with a 10.5m span, erected in 1855,
but for many years a county road southwards from Drumlonan has
crossed the canal here. In November 1968 the bridge collapsed under
the weight of a sand lorry and it was replaced in early 1971 by a high
single-span concrete structure with embanked approaches, erected by
Leitrim County Council.

31.28 Garadice Lough [Entry]. There are 3 consecutive pairs of entry
[32.12] markers past which the navigation course continues to the north of
the marked, centrally-placed Church Island. It then makes a RH
U-turn and rounds the Garadice Park headland, passing north of
Cherry Island. This lake is generally navigable though shallow at the
shorelines.

34.96 Garadice Lough [Exit].
[28.44]

35.02 Haughton's Shore Mooring [Ballinacur Harbour] [RH]. Entered to the
[28.38] RH, at the exit from Garadice Lough and some 140 metres short of
Ballinacur Bridge, this is a new harbour and a most welcome facility.
There are quite extensive quays, a boat slipway and a Service Block
with the range of facilities mentioned previously. This is a picturesque
mooring which will undoubtedly become very popular.

35.16 Ballinacur Road Bridge: No 24. A contractor working for County
[28.24] Leitrim Grand Jury erected this single masonry arch in 1854-5. It was
not one of the formal works belonging to the navigation, having its
origins as a county road bridge across an unaltered river. It carries the
Ballinamore/Killeshandra road.

35.25 Woodford Lough [Entry]. This is hardly more than a widening of the
[28.15] navigation on the right. It is just past Ballinacur Bridge.

35.42 Woodford Lough [Exit].
[27.98]

35.89 Ballymagauran [Ballymagovern] River Outfall [LH]. The river is not
[27.51] navigable and is marked by an 'End of Navigation' sign a little
upstream from the marked navigation channel.

36.38 Ballymagauran [Ballymagovern] Lough [Entry]. All three lakes in the
[27.02] chain here are in general unnavigable, outside the marked channel,
because of their pronounced shallowness.

37.01 Ballymagauran [Ballymagovern] Lough [Exit].
[26.39]

38.02 Derrycassan Lough [Entry].
[25.38]

39.03   Derrycassan Lough [Exit].
[24.37]

39.44   Coologe Lough [Entry].
[23.96]

39.93   Coologe Lough [Exit].
[23.47]

39.98   Coologe [Burren] Road Bridge: No 25. The present bridge and its road
[23.42]   approaches are completely new construction sited some 25m east of
         their predecessors. At the time of the original construction neither
         roadway nor bridge existed at this point; both were relatively recent.
         The new bridge is on a minor route from Bellaheady to Newtowngore.
         The replaced bridge was a low concrete structure.

40.63   Skelan [Kiltynaskellan] Lock: No 3. Here, from right to left, were
[22.77]   originally ranged across the channel a lock, large sluice, fish pass and
         weir. The lock was built in 1854-5. In 1855 it was reported that 'timber
         to raise the level of the water behind the weir, for the navigation to
         Aghoo, has been put on'. Opposite the lock [RH] was a lock house
         [erected in 1857]; it long ago disappeared. A footbridge across the weir
         gave access to the very remote site from the Coologe [west] side.

         The reconstruction involved major works at Kiltynaskellan, and a
         river diversion was carried out to facilitate progress. The Woodford
         River was given a new temporary course which looped past the site
         of the new weir [LH]. So impressive was the sight that it became a
         focal point for Sunday afternoon visitors, in spite of the relative
         isolation of the location. The new features across the waterway here
         are, again, lock [RH], fish pass and weir, parallel to which is a
         galvanized steel walkway. It may be noted that both the full name and
         its contraction, given above, have apparently gained official
         acceptance.

41.85   Callaghs Stream Outfall [RH]. An 'End of Navigation' sign marks the
[21.55]   entry of a tiny stream.

44.35   Bellaheady [Ballyheady] Road Bridge: No 26. This is a single masonry
[19.05]   arch of 13.7 metres span built in 1851-2. It carries a minor road to
         Ardlougher.

48.41   Crooked River Outfall [LH]. Entry point of a small tributary.
[14.99]

48.51   Derryginny: Cavan & Leitrim Railway Bridge [Site]. Now removed
[14.89]   completely, this was a low lattice-girder iron bridge, built in 1886-87,
         which would have obstructed boats. It carried the
         Ballinamore-Belturbet line of the narrow-gauge Cavan & Leitrim
         Railway [1887-1959] across the waterway. Clearly of little residual

scrap value, the bridge was only cleared away in 1992, 33 years after the rails were lifted.

49.05   Ballyconnell Mooring. Some 120m short of Ballyconnell Bridge is a
[14.35] substantial new concrete quay [LH]. On the quayside is a masonry
         Service Block, again with the full range of facilities. At the east end of
         the quay is the engineering base and machinery yard for maintenance
         of the river navigation. At the opposite end is a slipway for launching
         boats. Near this is a large granite boulder with a bilingual inscription
         commemorating the visit on 7 February 1992, to inspect progress on
         the reconstruction, of An Taoiseach, Mr C.J. Haughey.

The River Navigation:
Ballyconnell-Upper Lough Erne

49.17   Ballyconnell Road Bridge: No 27. This is a fine 2-arch masonry
[14.23] structure, built in 1849. Uniquely, it has a third, smaller, arch on the
         left for the tow-path, or 'horsewalk' as it was invariably referred to
         locally. It carries the Ballyconnell to Belturbet road.

49.21   Ballyconnell Wharf [LH]. This masonry-fronted quay is the third of
[14.19] those provided for the original navigation. About 35m long, it was
         provided with iron mooring posts when built in 1850.

49.46   Ballyconnell Weir [RH]. The weir is to the right of the navigation
[13.94] channel. It is provided with a steel walkway which forms part of a
         very pleasant circular walk from the town. At the same place was the
         old 1849-50 weir which incorporated a large sluice and a fish pass. The
         former was the only such sluice to be found on the canal in later years;
         it dated from 1931 and its continued existence was due to the mill.
         Beyond the weir, the river channel winds through the former
         Ballyconnell Demesne. Its only feature was an eel fishery with a set of
         regulating sluices built in 1852 as compensation for the removal of an
         older fishery. Some of the masonry still survives.

49.88   Ballyconnell Lock: No 2, and Accommodation Bridge: No 28. The new
[13.52] lock is at the location of its predecessor though slightly moved to the
         left. Across the east end of the lock is the new accommodation bridge.
         This is an additional feature, not a replacement. Immediately
         upstream of the lock [LH] is a short stub of waterway which heads
         towards the mills but stops at the boundary of the navigation
         property. It is aligned with the former mill head-race and could serve
         as a future source of water power at the mill complex.

         The original lock was built in 1849 and was the sole point on the
         navigation where a head of water was maintained [for the mills] for
         many years, latterly by a steel sluice gate erected in 1914 at its upper

end. Opposite the other end of the lock [LH] is the location of the former lock-house, a small [6.4m x 11.0m approx] single storey structure built in 1857. It was the only one of six to survive until the reconstruction.

Significant bank protection works were carried out below the lock where the river channel rejoined from the right, much rock armour being put in place to counter the effects of scour.

50.47   Ballyconnell Mill Tail-Race [LH]. There is an 'End of Navigation' sign
[12.93]   near the outfall of the old tailrace of the mills.

51.02   Scotchtown [Annagh] Island [West End; RH]. The channel divides,
[12.38]   navigation to the left, leaving the unnavigable branch to loop to the right around by Scotchtown Island, both ends of which are marked by 'End of Navigation' signs.

51.36   Scotchtown [Annagh] Island [East End; RH]. The channels rejoin at
[12.04]   the end of the island.

51.67   Cloncoohy Cut [Entry; LH]. The navigation enters Cloncoohy canal
[11.73]   cut which incorporates the tiny Cloncoohy Lough at its east end, a little way short of which the small Duvoge River enters. The unnavigable river channel is on the right and is marked at either end by 'End of Navigation' signs. [The navigation channel from the east end of the Cloncoohy Cut to the entry of the Dernagore is marked].

51.98   Cloncoohy Accommodation Bridge: No 29. The original 1855 bridge
[11.42]   was a three-span timber structure which became quite infamous in later years due to its dilapidated condition. It was replaced by a simple concrete structure around 1950, and the latter has since been superseded by a new 3-arch bridge.

52.65   Cloncoohy Cut [Exit; RH]. The navigation channel rejoins the river
[10.75]   which is on the right.

53.03   Dernagore Cut [Entry; LH]. Here begins a navigation cut, some 0.4
[10.37]   km long, the unnavigable river channel being on the right. Both ends of the cut are marked by 'End of Navigation' signs.

53.10   Dernagore Accommodation [Pontoon] Bridge. A post-Award
[10.30]   (latter-day) accommodation pontoon bridge across the navigation channel at Dernagore was removed in the reconstruction and not replaced.

53.43   Dernagore Cut Exit [RH]. The navigation channel rejoins the river
[09.97]   which is on the right.

54.30   Derrylaney River Outfall [LH]. An 'End of Navigation' sign marks the
[09.10]   entry of this small river.

55.08   Corraquill [Caroul] Lock: No 1, and Accommodation Bridge: No 30.
[08.32] The waterway splits, the left-hand being the navigation channel. The
        original lock was built in 1849. The new bridge spans the east end of
        the lock; it replaces an earlier concrete structure. The right-hand
        channel is spanned by a new weir [the original was built in 1852-3]
        which is protected by a barrier to prevent Erne-bound boats drawing
        too close. On the island, next to the lock was a two-storey toll
        collector's house built in 1857, the second of two; it had long since
        disappeared. It is not possible to cross the waterway by bridge or
        walkway at this point. The bridge gives access to the island only. The
        old alternative name, Caroul, which was very widely used, is a
        corruption of the local name 'Corrawaill'.

58.45   Aghalane Road Bridge [Ruins]: No 31. A three-arch masonry bridge
[04.95] was built in 1848-9 to replace an earlier inadequate structure. The
        central arch of the bridge (which was on the North/South
        [Fermanagh/Cavan] border) was demolished by an explosion in the
        early 1970s. Apart from the abutments the old bridge was cleared
        away and not replaced in the reconstruction.

58.95   Aghalane Mooring [Quay] [LH]. This is a new floating mooring,
[04.45] designed to allow boats to use it over a range of water levels (which
        can be high at times due to a back-up effect from Upper Lough Erne).
        It has a range of services for boats and a masonry Service Block
        housing laundry, showers and toilets has been provided. Sewage
        pumpout facilities are available.

60.18   Teemore [Corraback] Lough outfall [RH]. The lake, which is not
[03.22] navigable, is fed by the Rag River. There is an 'End of Navigation'
        marker at the outfall point.

61.45   Amoneen Lough outfalls [RH]. There are several narrow outfalls from
[01.95] this small unnavigable lake.

62.20   Anoneen Lough outfall [RH]. The lake is not navigable.
[01.20]

62.79   Drumard Lough outfall [RH]. The traveller to Belturbet will sail right
[00.61] through the marked north-west sector of Drumard Lough and then
        through the marked Foalies Cut (which was also dredged and
        improved by ESBI as part of the overall restoration programme).

63.40   Upper Lough Erne. The navigation terminates at the junction of the
[00.00] parishes of Galloon, Kinawley and Drumlane. The channel is well
        marked down past the outfalls of Anoneen and Drumard Loughs.

THE ERNE & LOUGH OUGHTER NAVIGATION
DRUMARD LOUGH TO BELTURBET

For the sake of completeness (and because many cruises will start or end at Belturbet) a short gazetteer is presented for the navigation from the Shannon-Erne Waterway, through Drumard Lough and Foalies Cut and then southwards along the Erne to Belturbet. The distances in open figures are a continuation of those from Leitrim; those in brackets are given from Belturbet. The designations [LH] and [RH] apply for a southbound trip. The 'Navigational Guide' to the Shannon-Erne Waterway covers the course from Drumard, via Foalies, to Belturbet.

Km

62.79 Drumard Lough [Entry; RH]. The course for Belturbet, which is
[06.26] marked, is south-easterly and fairly straight.

63.98 Drumard Lough [Exit]/Foalies Cut [Entry]. A pair of markers denotes
[05.07] the entry to the cut, which shortens the trip to Belturbet considerably.

64.27 Foalies Bridge. A single masonry arch.
[04.78]

64.52 Foalies Cut [Exit]/River Erne [RH]. Belturbet is to the right [south].
[04.53] Initially the course is without markers, but a series of markers
       commences about 1.5km from the Foalies Cut Exit.

66.72 Shancorry Lough Outfall [LH]. This is marked by an 'End of
[02.33] Navigation' sign.

67.78 Creeny Lough Outfall [LH]. This is marked by an 'End of Navigation'
[01.27] sign.

68.63 Creeny Bridge [LH]. There is an 'End of Navigation' sign at a bridge
[00.42] over a small stream. On the opposite bank of the Erne is the major
       cruiser base established by Emerald Star Line in 1993.

68.84 Belturbet Moorings [LH]. Modest moorings with a water supply are
[00.21] provided just past the Creeny Bridge sign.

69.05 River Erne: End of Navigation. A sign marks the end of the navigable
[00.00] waterway.

April 1994. Photo: Frank Miller, The Irish Times.

CHAPTER 8

CONCLUSION:
A PROMISING FUTURE

The restored navigation has been officially named 'The Shannon-Erne Water-way'; it is no longer the Ballinamore and Ballyconnell Canal. This is an excellent augury for the future, for it is surely as the key link between two great inland navigation systems that the waterway will come into its own. The nature and extent of the political and financial support for its restoration underlines its future prominence as a vital part of the most extensive inland waterway leisure ground in Europe. Its former designation could not begin to convey its potential importance for tourism development North and South and for the revitalization of the area through which it runs.

Although conceived as a 'Shannon-Erne' link 150 years ago, hopes of its success in this regard had been dashed before its completion — the com-pletion of the trunk lines in the railway network eliminated the need for a more leisurely form of Belfast-Limerick connection. And, sadly, it was to turn out that even as a local 'Ballinamore and Ballyconnell Canal' there was no success to be had for such a transport artery in a poor region where the hoped-for benefits of the Arigna and Creevelea coal and iron industries never materialized.

And the future for the Shannon-Erne Waterway? All the indications are that this will be very successful. It is being confidently marketed with funds provided by the International Fund for Ireland and the tourist boards, North and South. An extremely attractive brochure has been produced showing the waterway to great advantage. A complementary brochure, imaginatively titled 'Cruise the North West Passage' has been issued by Emerald Star Line Ltd, one of the major cruise hire lines on the Shannon system, which has indicated its commitment to the new link by the opening of an elaborate new cruiser base on the Erne at Belturbet. There is a high degree of local commit-ment to the waterway with, for example, planned pleasure trips on Lough

Scur, projected marinas at Leitrim Village and in Ballinamore, and cruising holidays by barge.

Although cost benefit analyses have shown that the anticipated economic advantages to the region served by the waterway, and indeed to tourism in general, considerably outstrip the great cost of the restoration, the viewer leaning over a bridge, or sitting beside a lock, might be forgiven for wondering 'was it worth it?' By any yardstick the answer is a resounding and unequivocal yes. To study any of the multiple works and features of the navigation is to discover just how superb is the waterway that has been recreated. It is an example, perhaps unique, of how well an extremely complex project, with its drainage, engineering, social and other implications, can be carried out given the correct expertise and skills — in both planning and execution — and, most important of all, the proper funding.

Major Lefroy's comment of 1923, despite its geographical inexactitude, has at last gained credibility — this *is* the finest canal in this island.

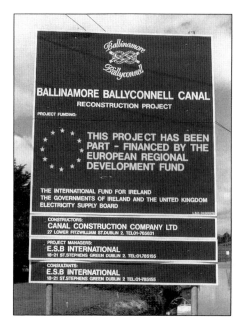

Left: On the Shannon-Erne Waterway, 1994.
Photo: Frank Miller, The Irish Times.
Below: Notice of official opening

NOTICE

The Office of Public Works, Dublin and The Department of Agriculture, Northern Ireland announce that the recently reconstructed SHANNON-ERNE WATERWAY will be open to the public from Saturday, 2nd April, 1994.

Locks and other services along the Waterway are operable by a card system. Cards priced, £10 each, will be available from the above date at Killarcan Lock (near Leitrim Village) and at the Tourist Information Office at Enniskillen. Navigation Charts are also available, price £7 each.

Enquiries to:

The Office of Public Works	The Department of Agriculture
51 St. Stephen's Green	The Mall West
Dublin 2	Armagh BT69 9BL
Telephone 01-6613111	0861-522774

OPW

Oifig na nOibreacha Poiblí
The Office of Public Works